Pro Uita Monastica

Pro Vita Monastica

AN ESSAY IN DEFENCE OF THE CONTEMPLATIVE VIRTUES BY HENRY DWIGHT SEDGWICK

AUTHOR OF "LIFE OF MARCUS AURELIUS," "DANTE," "AN APOLOGY FOR OLD MAIDS," "ITALY IN THE THIRTEENTH CENTURY," "A SHORT HISTORY OF ITALY," &c.

BOSTON
The Atlantic Monthly Press
MDCCCCXXIII

D. B. UPDIKE · THE MERRYMOUNT PRESS · BOSTON
PRINTED IN THE UNITED STATES OF AMERICA

In Memoriam

Tu, che vedi i miei mali indegni ed empi,
  Re del cielo, invisibile, immortale,
  Soccorri all' alma disviata e frale,
  E'l suo difetto di tua grazia adempi:
Si che, s' io vissi in guerra ed in tempesta,
  Mora in pace ed in porto; e se la stanza
  Fu vana, almen sia la partita onesta.
A quel poco di viver che m'avanza
  Ed al morir degni esser tua man presta
  Tu sai ben che n'altrui non ho speranza.

Petrarch

Loquar ad Dominum meum cum sim pulvis et cinis.

Thomas à Kempis

Fili, non potes perfectam possidere libertatem, nisi totaliter abneges temetipsum.

Thomas à Kempis

                              Man shall find grace;
And shall not grace find means, that finds her way,
The speediest of thy winged messengers,
To visit all thy creatures?

Milton

Rien ne donne le repos que la recherche sincère de la vérité.

Pascal

Table of Contents

Preface

T is common for persons who may be classed as indifferent concerning religious matters, to find fault with current Christianity, at least as it shows itself in Protestant churches, to speak slightingly of it, saying that Christianity has lost its hold upon the people, does not lead in matters of conduct nor in ideal purposes, does not produce any radiant personalities or examples of heroic self-sacrifice, does not persuade people that its conceptions of truth concerning the ultimate ends and meaning of life can be of any significance to them, does not help in the solution of social problems — in short, that Christianity has become a laggard, a tagger-on to society, a hindrance to freedom of thought and action, serving as an excuse for self-content to those who find themselves well off in the existing state of things and are really unconcerned about the soul.

Nor is that the only sort of criticism to which Christianity lies open. During the war, it was plain enough that in each of the warring countries religion had been cast afresh in the ancient mould of a tribal god. And for years before the war, many religious-minded persons regarded ecclesiastical Christianity as a sort of hardening of the spirit that hindered the free play of human hopes for a better world.

I have no concern with the justice or injustice of such criticisms, I merely note that they are widespread and are uttered nowadays even more by persons who believe in Christianity as a factor for spiritual good than by those who do not, and further that these fault-finders, so far as I know, are in full accord with the most devout Christians in the belief that Christ taught the most direct, possibly the only, way toward the goal of spiritual endeavor, which he called the Kingdom of Heaven.

Preface

It would be quite beside my purpose to treat such great questions as to what truth there may be in Christianity, whether of fact or symbol, or as to whether it is for the good of mankind that Christianity, organized as it is, should continue; I merely wish to lay stress upon the fact that, for one reason and another, Christianity, at least among Protestants, has cast aside, or dropped out, a great part of the ancient practices that during many centuries helped it adapt itself to human needs, enabled it to produce heroic and radiant personalities, and shed over it a poetry which it now lacks. I refer to the practices of withdrawal from the world of ordinary life and from the usual occupations of men, into some solitary or sequestered place, where in hermitage or monastery they might give themselves up to contemplation, meditation, and prayer, and to such labors in library or garden as should best fit the mind to be the dwelling-place of what-

ever thoughts might seem to them the highest, best, and most beautiful.

And as, to my way of thinking, such sequestered habits and practices are of the essence of Christianity, for without them it goes about its tasks halt and maimed, in hopeless inadequacy, so also I believe that the individual life, unless it take advantage of those practices, withdrawing apart to think high thoughts, and to reconsider by the light of such thoughts its hopes, ambitions, and desires, is and must be imperfect.

The mass of men are absorbed in animal existence and indifferent to such matters; but there are always a few, bewildered by the "burden of the mystery," who would like to set forth in quest of the spiritual life. I do not suggest the literal revival of ancient monasticism; I counsel no one to set out for the Thebaid or Monte Cassino, St. Gall or Cîteaux. The seeker need go no further than to an upper chamber in his own

*dwelling or to a secluded corner of his own gar-
den, or to any other place where, by means of
such accompaniments as suit retirement,— books,
flowers, music, meditation, prayer,— a man
may refresh his spirit and wash the dust from
his soul, whether his retirement be for half an
hour a day, or to a retreat for a week once a
year, or, if he be so minded and his situation
permits, for such proportion of his time as shall
best prosper him upon his spiritual quest.*

*Until recently this doctrine of a retreat with
its attendant circumstances had been one of the
chief teachings of the Church. Throughout the
Middle Ages Christianity asserted the superior-
ity of the contemplative life over the active life.
Dante, the noblest voice of Christian tradition,
says: " In this life we can have two kinds of happiness by following two different roads, both good
and excellent— one road is the Active Life, by
which we may attain to a fair state of happi-*

ness, the other is the Contemplative Life, and that leads us to supreme felicity." It is difficult to see how religious teaching could do otherwise than give the palm to the contemplative life. At best, in the active life the mind can but busy itself with good works, it never can escape from this world of sense, of imprisoning space and temporal bonds; whereas in contemplation, the mind—such was the Christian doctrine—soars above the world of creatures into an ethical quietude, where in self-forgetfulness it becomes at one with God, or if that be denied it, at least it attains to peace with itself. But in our time the Church is no longer the proud possessor of truth and power that she was in centuries past, she no longer goes her own way, knowing that the world will follow: she has become timid, apprehensive lest the world abandon her altogether, so she goes as the world goes, and does as the world does. " She that was great among the nations, and princess among

Preface

the provinces, how is she become tributary!" And so, she has wholly reversed the judgment of the Middle Ages and cast the doctrine of the contemplative life, of monasticism, of a secluded existence devoted to prayer and meditation, and all such notions, into the limbo of outworn things.

It is in this ready surrender to the imperious activity of a world hungry for pleasure and material enjoyments, that the Church I think has made her great mistake. She has sealed up the fountain entrusted to her, she neither speaks the word nor smites the rock to make the waters of spiritual refreshment burst forth. She is converting Christianity into a business of social reform, taking on the restless activity of the world. And she affects to regard the change as a matter for self-congratulation. She is pleased that she has broken down the old distinction between the religious and the secular life, that she is keeping abreast of the times, that she has done this and

[xv]

that which the world deems desirable, and that
by so doing she satisfies the spiritual needs of her
members, forgetting that the business of Christianity is not merely to satisfy the spiritual needs
that she finds, but also to deepen and broaden and
heighten those that exist, and to create new needs
as well.

To the outsider, however, it is plain that the
Church has not made this radical change of her
own volition; she has yielded to the importunate
and the worldly. The triumph of the active virtues over the contemplative is not a triumph of
religion but of the world, just as the great social
and political revolution in the fourth century,
which text-books upon history call the victory of
Christianity, was also in reality the triumph of
the world over religion. And if Christianity is to
turn about again and lead, if not the many, at
least the few that seek the spiritual life, she must
supplement her active virtues with the contem-

plative virtues and the practice of them, and enlarge her ideal of service with the notion that to meditate upon things divine until all lesser desires fall away is to render a service to men at least equal to those rendered by the active virtues.

My purpose in this little book is limited to a consideration of the rift between the world and the religious spirit, as it has existed throughout the course of Christianity and exists still; the thesis being that the contemplative life, by which I mean the definite and regular practice of meditation, prayer, and the restriction of one's society to books and flowers, for certain times, is necessary for that serenity of spirit which is now and always has been the chief need of mankind; for upon serenity of spirit depends our power to see truth, to do justice, and to think no evil.

H. D. S.

March, 1923

Pro Uita Monastica

I

The World and the Recluse

The world is too much with us.
Wordsworth

 SOCIETY depends for its well-being upon an ability to make use of its latent energy. In time of war most societies, such as our own nation, develop a power to draw upon moral and mental resources of all kinds, of which, in times of ease, they had not been aware. Physical danger has a magic virtue, it doubles the strength of the strong, the craft of the cunning, and the nobility of the noble. This is the one good that can be ascribed to war. But in times of peace the reservoirs of devotion, self-sacrifice, and heroism empty themselves into the dry sands of ordinary life, and the power of setting an idea high above all material things fades like a mirage. One of the chief problems of social life is how to find, and how to put to use, whatever spiritual forces there may be in individuals. It is a religious problem and as such should belong to organized Christianity. But many people have lost faith in Christianity, at least in its modern Protestant form. They con-

[3]

sider Christian communities both at home and
abroad, and are forced to conclude that our professed religion renders little or no spiritual service; the more radical go so far as to regard it
as a wholly unsuccessful experiment, while even
the more conservative believe that, somehow or
other, it has lost access to a reservoir of strength
that it once possessed.

My thesis then is, that the fate of Christianity lies in its power to recover, and make use of,
those resources of the spirit from which in earlier
times it drew innocence, peace, serenity, and joy.
And as the way to recover those qualities, that
ancient Christian poise and radiance of spirit, is
neither smooth nor easy, an attempt to consider
the nature of the road pursued by men who in
the past attained their goal, as well as the causes
that may impel others to-day to undertake the
quest, may not be amiss, especially if the attempt
be made in the hope that those Christians who
are concerned over the fate of Christianity may
help and encourage such seekers on their way.

Among the many lines of demarcation that
divide men, that one to which I wish to address
myself creates two classes of very unequal size.

One class comprises all people who lead what
it is usual to call normal lives, men and women

[4]

who take their places in the fabric of the social whole as a matter of course, both in the workroom and the playground of life; who seek out other people, set store by acquaintances, do business with one another, enter upon joint enterprises, join guilds and clubs, cultivate curiosity concerning their fellows, and in every way look upon themselves primarily as members of a social organism. Such people, taken together, constitute the *World*. The other class comprises those persons who, for one reason or another, whether native disposition or the experiences of life, shun human relationships, slink away from their fellows, and seek to loosen all the ties by which life without their doing has bound them to the World: in short, to live, so far as may be practicable, by themselves and to themselves.

A division into classes marked by such contrasting opinions implies antagonism; but there has been and is more antagonism between the World and the recluse than the mere acceptance of opposing ideals necessarily implies. This is due partly to historical causes, but chiefly because the contrast between their opposing ideals is sharper and of a higher emotional pitch than usually happens between differing categories.

The World professes liberality, a desire to

leave every man free to pursue his own ideals
according to his own lights. But in practice the
World finds this maxim too difficult to carry
out, and by open reproach or secret slur con-
demns the recluse for abandoning what, according to the World's way of thinking, are the
social duties of all men. It would be a good thing
if liberty to pursue their ideals were granted to
all men. Life as a whole is richer according to
the measure of its diversities; for each man who
endeavors to bring his life into conformity with
his own ideal must perforce contribute something to the general good. The sum of ideals
that men strive after constitutes the true wealth
of mankind. The social whole, whether the recluse likes it or not, is a unity; and anyone
who seriously seeks to live his own life to his
own highest satisfaction necessarily renders the
greatest social service in his power. This is obvious; and in matters that do not touch its *amour
propre* the World encourages diversity, or at least
follows its principle of giving to each man his
liberty. There may be differences of taste, but
open disapprobation of a contrary taste is rarely
present. One man may feel inwardly certain that
his ways of living and doing are better than the
ways of his neighbor, nevertheless he does not

proceed to the logical complement of his thought
and decry the opposite ways of living and doing.
But in the disagreement between the World and
the recluse an element of hostility bristles up.
The cause is plain. The recluse has turned his
back upon the World because he does not like
the World, and the World takes umbrage and
stigmatizes his departure as desertion. The two
views of life are opposites, mutually exclusive,
like heat and cold, and the only way to recon-
cile them is by some hypothesis of a more comprehensive whole that shall include them both,
as a full day includes both noontide and the
night.

The World is busy with work and pleasure;
early and late it toils and sweats; it sows and
reaps; it converts forest into pasture and swamp
into cornfield; it digs a thousand hidden substances out of the depths of the earth; it builds
ships, railroads, cities; it stirs up individuals,
communities, nations, to greater and greater economic effort; and it makes war. In short, what
the World does is so stupendous that it may
well be excused for feeling sure that its way of
life is better and nobler than that of the recluse.
In its more emotional moments the World asserts that it is performing the part ascribed by

Neoplatonic philosophy to emanations from
divinity, that it is weaving *der Gottheit lebendiges
Kleid*, and it holds, as a corollary to this belief,
that the recluse is a shirk, a slacker, a deserter
from the efforts and hardships of the actual, practical living of life.

One must keep in mind an obvious criticism
upon the World's position. It is this: The
World's opinion springs directly from its activities. The World acts upon impulses, appetites,
instincts, and the customs that they have set up.
It has been moulded on the wheel of the master
potter, Desire. It glorifies life, not through any
process of reasoning, but from the mere exhilaration of the rush of tumultuous existence. Each
man believes himself a rational being; but in the
clutch of desire the human reason is no more
than a puppet. The will-to-live cracks its whip,
and the World dances. Under the intoxicating
influence of the god of life, men hurrah and
shout that his gift is good, and praise its protean
manifestations; they sing soft or loud, bass or
treble, according as the breath of life blows
through the human pipes. There are, no doubt,
individuals, here and there, who strive to preserve the independence of reason and attempt
to control conduct; but cowboys afoot might as

well try to stop a stampede of maddened steers
as the reasoning few to guide the course of the
multitude.

And this will-to-live has taken a social form.
Psychologists tell us that speech, morality,
knowledge, the very consciousness of self, exist
because the power that expresses itself in life
has fashioned creatures of the human species for
mutual dependence. It is inevitable that the mass
of men who constitute the World should hold
a social creed and believe in a communal, cheek-
by-jowl, organization of society, in which every
man at roll-call shall answer *adsum* and take his
place in the social fabric. For, the faster life
moves, the more potent human energy becomes,
the greater the power it acquires through science
and coöperation, so much the more firmly does
the World believe in the closer and closer union
of men. And at the present time, more than
ever before, the World is out of sympathy with
the motives and aspirations that govern the recluse; more than ever it is confident in its own
views and ideals, more and more impatient of
criticism, more and more disinclined to open its
mind to alien values and alien modes of thought.
Its conception of virtue has become purely social, and through its professed ideals of *service*

and *social justice* it colors its condemnation of the
recluse with righteous indignation.

On the other hand, it must be admitted that
the recluse is not free from prejudice. By leaving
the World he has not merely condemned it, but
he has also openly proclaimed his condemnation. In his heart he looks upon the World as
he would upon the train of Bacchanals that once
followed Dionysus over the Thracian hills, men
and women with hair flying, clad in fawn skins,
crowned with ivy, waving the thyrsus, singing
wild melodies, and madly dancing to pipe and
cymbal, all worshiping their beautiful young god,
whose magic and mystery had set them beside
themselves with enthusiasm. In the World's
ways the recluse sees nothing but the will-to-live,
attended by desire, appetite, impulse, emotion,
leading its votaries in a mad dance over a wild
road from birth to death.

This is an extravagant and unjust view of the
World, and shows how hard it is to judge justly
where there is an emotional opposition between
opinions. Yet all contraries may be reconciled if
we will but devise a synthesis large enough to
include them; and my purpose is to justify the
recluse by the contention that a reconciliation
between the World's values and his may be found

by uniting them together in a larger conception
of human interests. My belief is that the recluse
serves humanity, and thereby serves the World,
quite as much as the World serves the recluse.
And I shall hope to justify that belief by indicat-
ing the path which leads the recluse to his solitude, and by an exposition of his sequestered
and cloistered occupations; for at each stage, as
I think, he does not withdraw further, but rather
comes closer and closer to the dearest interests of
humanity.

The recluse of whom I speak and whose cause
I support is, I admit, somewhat of a fanatic;
but there is little danger lest there be many such,
and fanaticism is often necessary in order to clear
the way for those of less resolute purpose who
would be glad to avail themselves in modera-
tion of what the fanatics insist upon to excess. It
may be that only the violence of fanaticism can
restore the contemplative virtues to the esteem
in which they were held of old, bring back meditation to its place in the ritual of Christianity,
enfranchise the moderate recluse, and enable him
to withdraw from the World for a fortnight a
year, for a day in the month, or an hour in the
day.

II

Disillusion

E vidi questo globo
Tal, ch' io sorrisi del suo vil sembiante.
Paradiso, xxii, 134, 135

HE first stage on this road to spiritual freedom is the consciousness of a great change. The seeker awakes to find all his values shriveled and shrunken. He is like the sojourner in a foreign land who returns after long years to his native village to find the houses all standing as they were, ranged each in its curtilage along the village street, the elms and maples rooted to their ancient places and glorious as of old in ten thousand shimmering leaves, the gardens blooming in many colors, and all the outward lineaments of the beloved place seemingly as they used to be; but the soul of house and garden, the spirit that gave them life, the boys and girls, the loving friends, the hospitable hosts, the welcome, and the cheer—where are they? Like this sojourner who walks sadly up and down, bewildered to find the husks all permanent yet empty of fruit, so the man that has awakened to find the values of life all topsy-turvy, walks to and fro in bewildered contemplation.

Those values had seemed so solid. Wrought and fashioned out of daily experience, they had been grouped and classified, very much as the data of sense are dealt with; and just as the data of sense are compounded into the system of science, so those values, also, had been built up into a system of ethics. And yet the old values are now become as insipid as the white of an egg. The cause or occasion of this change may have been bereavement, disappointment, sickness, old age, or philosophy, but whatever it may have been, its effect has been to convert the treasure-house of the World into a closet of vanities. Here starts the beginning of the new road, passing through the portal of disillusion.

. The World's prizes — fame, good report, distinction, titles, offices, honors — which up to now looked so fair and shining, things which the seeker had been taught to treat with deference and speak of with praise — what has happened? How are the lights that lighted them grown dim! Where is the sparkle and the gold? The bewildered seeker rubs his eyes. Has he, unbeknown to himself, been initiated into some great mystery, whereby desire and admiration have dropped away, leaving him so indifferent that if he could put out his hand and take all these honors, he would not lift a finger? Perhaps in the depths of his subconsciousness, where the Puck-like spirit of self-love is said to play its most impish tricks, jealousy, the impulse to decry what one cannot get,—*les raisins sont verts et bons pour des goujats,*—has been able to deceive him, but with his waking consciousness he is all unaware of deception. To read one's name on the front page of the morning paper, to be on the lips of thousands, to be applauded by countless hands,—are these the guerdons that satisfy ambitious men? And the multitude that read, cheer, clap, what are they? What is their approval worth? And where and who are the notable men praised and cheered yesterday, and yesterday's yesterday?

And as with ambitions, so with possessions. A fog falls thick and dark about them. They loom up like icebergs at night before the watch on the deck of a fishing smack; what profit have they? A palace in New York, a gallery adorned with famous paintings, drawing-rooms furnished forth by Adam, Sheraton, Riesener, and Gouthière, stables, a yacht, a box at the opera, a troop of servants, and all the luxuries that wealth can buy? Certainly the seeker is not aware of envy,

nor of any sentiment except of freedom and
thankfulness. So with all the inventory that the
Prince of this World might unroll. The seeker
realizes that all his relations with things of this
sort are changed. He need not stuff his ears with
wax or lash himself to the mast; the song of these
sirens is out of tune and harsh.

Like a pilgrim of old bound for the Holy
Land, he takes his staff and goes, but not in
anger or in contempt, rather in bewilderment and
in discontent with himself, oppressed by a shal-
low breathing and a sultry air.

III
The Voice of Authority

Τεκνία, φυλάξατε ἑαυτοὺς ἀπὸ τῶν εἰδώλων.
3 Epistle of St. John, v:21

HE portal that leads out of the World is disillusion. Having passed through, the pilgrim is an exile and must seek a new home. What shall he do? Where shall he go? In the forefront of all maxims that look to conduct stands the Delphic command, "Know thyself"; but how shall the pilgrim know himself? for the ordinary terms of self-explanation fail him. He has no part in the hopes, likings, and customs of other men and cannot measure himself by them. He is aware of unlikenesses, but not of likeness. Knowledge of self can be but ill-expressed in negatives. What is there about himself that cuts him off, in what seems to him most essential, from his fellows? He is one of the multitudinous human units that have been fashioned by the patient processes of nature, by the push of vital energy, by the caprices of selection, by the unnumbered influences that act upon organic matter. Men have been shaped by mutual action and reaction, and finally compounded into

our social fabric. These processes have not only
made the World what it is, but also each man
what he is; they have determined his thought,
language, ethics, knowledge, personality. Why,
then, is the pilgrim so different from his fellows?
Is he, as the World judges, deficient in social
capacity? Is it an inability to hold his own in the
struggle for life that the spirit of self-love has
disguised under a cloak of mystery? Is it sub-
conscious repulsion from noise, coarseness, and
vanity? Or is there some law of variability that
creates in the World creatures that are not really
of it? Or has some foreign element been at work
undermining the labor of its fellow elements?
And, if so, what is its nature? Can it be that a
power from a spiritual sphere, some $\delta\alpha\iota\mu\omega\nu$, some
invisible messenger, takes a few by the hand and
bids them arise and forsake the World? The psychological causes, no doubt, are clear to the psy-
chologist, but to the pilgrim self-analysis yields
little. And so he turns to see what other men, in
like situation with himself, have done in the past.

The sense of disillusion, of dissatisfaction
with the World, is no new thing. It is old, very
old, and therefore he to whom it comes is able
to question the experience of others at different
places along the road of human history, in the

hope that what others have found restorative may be of help also to him. A glance at the pages of the past shows that many, many persons, in their disillusion and discontent, have withdrawn themselves apart from the ordinary ways of men, and that they did so under a deep sense of antagonism between the standards and values of the World and certain ideal standards and values which, as they thought, if believed in, would make life intelligible.

This antagonism these precursors have defined in various ways, as between the World and the Spirit; between the life of the senses and that of the soul; between illusion and truth. It is not of much consequence how the two terms are defined, whether the World means the world of ordinary human life or the domination of the baser appetites and ambitions; whether the soul is a reality, an abstraction, or a symbol; or what illusion, and what truth, may be; the matter of importance is the profound antagonism between the old values and the new. It is upon this antagonism that the greatest religious teachers have built their doctrines.

In the Gospel of St. John the World is set in opposition to the Spirit of Truth: "I will pray the Father, and he shall give you another Com-

forter, that he may abide with you for ever; even
the Spirit of truth; whom the world cannot receive, because it seeth him not, neither knoweth
him. . . . If ye were of the world, the world
would love his own: but because ye are not of
the world, but I have chosen you out of the
world, therefore the world hateth you. . . . When
the Comforter is come . . . he will reprove the
world of sin . . . because they believe not on
me. . . . Be of good cheer; I have overcome the
world. . . . O righteous Father, the world hath
not known thee: but I have known thee. . . ."

These are the words of religious mysticism;
they belong, many people would think, to another time and another race, and perhaps they
convey little meaning to rationalistic minds; but
at least they proclaim, with the emotional power
of poetic imagination, the existence of something
which men, in default of a more definite term,
call holy, something which stands in sharp opposition to the ordinary ways of men. Philo the
Jew says: "It is just as impossible that the love
of the World can coexist with the love of God,
as for light and darkness to coexist at the same
time with one another."

Subsequently, bigoted men set against each
other soul and body, in order to express as for-

cibly as possible this contrast of values. This
opposition is misleading and unfortunate, and
proves the drying up of spiritual imagination.
It was adopted because it served the immediate
purpose of convenience in proselytizing, of de-
manding from neophytes mere effortless comprehension, and, once adopted, it swept aside all
metaphysical delicacy of interpretation. Soul and
body, instead of taking their places as supple-
mentary and coöperative collaborators with different tasks, were set in antagonism to one another as opposites and enemies. But this error
should not prejudice us against the plain distinction between the two theories of value.

A more just and sensible interpretation of the
relation was adopted by the Greeks, who empha-
sized the difference between the material things
with which the bodily senses are primarily busy
and those spiritual things with which the sensi-
bilities of the soul were believed to concern
themselves. Socrates busied himself with this
difference on the day of his death. He was sit-
ting on his couch in the prison; at times he
rubbed his leg that had been chafed by the fetters, and at times he stroked the head of his
well-beloved disciple, Phædo, and in his talk
he said: "Shall we assume that there are two

kinds of things, one that can be seen, and the
other without material form, and that that which
has no material form is always the same and that
which can be seen always changing; and that we
are made up of body and soul and the body
resembles rather that which is visible, while the
soul resembles rather that which has no material form? Well, then, we have been saying for a
long time that when the soul makes use of the
body to investigate anything, by means of sight
or hearing or any other of the senses, — for to
investigate by means of the senses signifies by
means of the body, — then she is dragged by the
body into the region of things that are never
stable, and wanders about and gets confused and
dizzy, as if she were drunk, because she asso-
ciates with these unstable things. But when the
soul, of herself, alone, ponders and reflects, then
she passes into a region of purity, eternity, im-
mortality, and unchangeableness, and, since she
too is of such nature that she is at home there,
she abides there (when she is alone by herself
and not hindered) and she rests from her wandering, and with that which never changes she
remains unchanging, because she has laid hold
of the eternal things. And this condition of the
soul is called wisdom."

Socrates, as well as St. John and Philo, lived in a far-off time, unfurnished with the speculations and classified experience which have wrought so great a change in our attitude toward the metaphysical world. The data and assumptions on which they base their philosophies have little in common with the data and assumptions on which we base ours. But the difference between that part of man which concerns itself with physical appetites and that other part which loves to dwell among those high abstractions, which some men in their passionate yearning call spiritual realities, remains as broad and deep as ever.

The like antithesis, only still more fundamental, appears in Buddha's teaching. He left home, wife, luxury, the prospect of authority and power, all the things that the World sets store by, in order to discover a standard of values that should be the very opposite of that which he had been taught. And an integral part of the story of Christ, of Buddha, of Socrates, is the paradox, that the veneration and worship accorded to them by a great part of mankind was given for the very reason that they forsook and denounced, both in their lives and their teachings, the standards of ordinary mankind, and set up other standards of a wholly contradictory character.

III

The Value of Precedent

Mundo erant alieni, sed Deo proximi ac familiares amici.
Thomas à Kempis

HE seeker, convert, or novice as we may call him, even if he be not ready to proffer submission, can-not but entertain respect for voices which, in spite of the innovations of time, in spite of science and a multitude of philosophers, are still the most authoritative in history; for the voice of greatest authority is that which speaks most directly to the ear of our deep-est emotional need. In the realm of speculation upon the things of sense, hypothesis has suc-ceeded hypothesis, and stability is at best a recent acquisition; but in the realm of values that de-termine the worth of life, there has been for all generations of men with like needs as ourselves a sensitive needle that has steadily pointed in a direction away from the World. The credulous believe that it points to the very central light of the universe — *Deus illuminatio mea* — but the novice need do no more than to accept its di-rection. Some hypothesis he must adopt or he will but go at random. As one of the speakers in

[23]

the *Phædo* says: " I think it is either impossible
or very difficult to know about these things in
this life; and yet not to investigate them in every
way, to desist from inquiry before I am tired
out, would be the mark of a feeble fellow. We are
obliged to do one of two things, either to find
out what is the truth about these matters, or, if
that is impossible, we must take the best rational
theory, the hardest to refute, get aboard it as if
it were a raft, and sail through the dangers of
life—unless we should be able to make our voyage in greater safety upon a stauncher vessel,
I mean by means of some divine revelation."

These authoritative voices, then, bid the
seeker turn his back upon the World. That is
strong doctrine; for in its fullness it would mean
to withdraw from familiar things, from daily
usages, from the ties and entanglements of social
and business life, from habitual companionship, in
short, almost, as the Bible says, to be born again.
Certainly no novice would interpret the voice
of authority in that comprehensive fashion. He
would, perhaps, grasp at some figurative meaning, such as to retire into his inner self. Marcus
Aurelius says: "Nowhere can a man go to find
peace more abundantly or greater freedom from
the cares of the world, than in his own soul. Re-

tire thither often and refresh thy spirit." But the
novice will surely find that mere retirement in
thought is not sufficient to give his spirit ease,
so long as his eyes behold vanity all about and
his ears are exposed to the perpetual clamour of
people praising the things of the World.

Nevertheless, circumstances alter cases, and
whereas in the fourth century the novice might
have gone forth eagerly from Antioch, let us say,
into the deserts of Syria, or in a later century
from Rome to Monte Cassino, or later still from
Paris to Cîteaux, to-day he would hesitate long
to leave his world of New York, or Boston, without some overpowering inducement. At least,
bare prudence would suggest that he should first
examine and consider what had happened to
men who had fled from the World. So, let us
suppose, bearing in mind that the antagonism
between the World and what Socrates regarded
as spiritual wisdom is constant, however the conception of those two terms may change their
meanings — let us suppose the seeker to interest himself in what happened to these men of old
whom we may call, according to our bias, fugitives from the World or pioneers of the spiritual
life.

Eugénie de Guérin wrote in her diary: "This

is the day of Saint Pachomius, the father of
monks. I have just read his life; it is very beautiful. These lives of solitaries have a charm for
me! Most of all, those that can be imitated. The
others one admires, like the pyramids. As a rule,
one always finds something good in them when
one reads wisely, even in their extreme exaggerations; theirs were heroic feats that tend to make
us devout, and to admire what is high.''

Eugénie de Guérin was a recluse, both in spirit
and in life. Her brother, her father, her books,
—St. François de Sales, Thomas à Kempis, and
such,—her journal, her bird, her dog, the parish
church, the poor peasants round about, constituted her world. And yet, to this recluse in "the
solitude of Cayla" the earliest of the Christian
monks, who established his primitive monastery
in the deserts of Egypt, was a light and a guide.
As the bee carries the pollen from the flower on
the hilltop to the flower in the valley, so there
is some winged communication between those
who serve the same ideal, however remote their
respective places and their respective times,
borne onward as it were upon vibrations of some
spiritual ether. It is common to speak of anchorites and monks as if they cut all communica-
tions, broke all relations, between themselves and

their fellow men. But a very slight acquaintance with their lives shows that this is not so; they substituted new relations for the old. From their deserts and monastic walls they have exerted a greater influence over the lives of men than if they had stayed in the places of their birth and followed the customs of their townsfolk. And it is just because they lived all their lives in solitude or seclusion that they succeeded in teaching the Church in their day, that the relation of cause and effect does exist between withdrawal from the world and that habit of serenity which is the nurse of purity, compassion, and justice.

Ⰼ
Saint Anthony

Know ye not that the friendship of the world is enmity with God? Whosoever therefore will be a friend of the world is the enemy of God.
St. James, iv: 4

AINT Pachomius founded the first Christian monastery; but St. Anthony was the first Christian hermit, and in the popular mind stands as the conspicuous example of the type. Times change, and with them the customs and usages of men. Dogmas, creeds, ideals pass away, but the human heart remains to-day very much as it was in St. Anthony's time, and it would be as hazardous to say that his experience of life, his way of bringing his soul to peace, and his way of benefiting his fellow men, can be of no present service, as it would be to shut the pages of Plato on the ground that the world is so changed that his thoughts can no longer stimulate our imagination in its task of guiding our feet along our paths to-day.

The chief difference between St. Anthony's World and ours lies in this, that our World is far more comely and seductive, far more bedizened and tempting, as he would have said, and

[28]

therefore there are far fewer who seek to leave it. St. Anthony was like Christian in *Pilgrim's Progress* fleeing the City of Destruction. He turned his back upon the World and betook himself to the solitude of the desert. *Ipse jam omnibus sæculi vinculis liber asperum atque arduum arripuit institutum* — free from all the fetters of the World he laid stout hold of his harsh and arduous purpose. To most people to-day St. Anthony was a fanatic, who gave himself over to unpleasant, superstitious, and foolish practices. Such a judgment implies ignorance and also a sluggish imagination. "Forests are delightful," says the disciple of Buddha; "where the World takes no delight there the passionless take delight, for they seek not pleasure." And in the solitude of the desert, as in that of the forest, there is always one denizen, the spirit of Poetry. She takes her pleasure in the silence of waste places, seeking communion with quiet, broken only by the whispering wind or the multitudinous soft noises that little creatures make. The desert is very beautiful; there light decks the earth with its most enchanting hues, and more than elsewhere turns color into symbols of things invisible; and there the heated air hums a magical melody to the spiritual ear. The children of the World

turn poetry into prose; and more than that, they
not only fail to get the meaning of the solitary
life, but they falsify, or distort to an extent that
is equivalent to falsification. Of this unfairness,
which is due to prejudice, the life of St. Anthony
offers an example. The one incident in the saint's
life that the World knows is what it calls "The
Temptation of St. Anthony," and from the stress
that has been laid upon this incident by painter
and novelist, the usual inference is that the poor
saint all his life was obsessed by images of cour-
tezans. This is because the World interests itself
in such matters and recks little of the long drudg-
ery by which hermits and monks attained to
dominion over the impulses of the body. The
principal record of St. Anthony is a biography
ascribed to Athanasius, the famous theologian,
which contains about sixty ordinary pages. The
passage that relates the incident in question is,
in the Latin version, "*Ille [diabolus] per noctes
in pulchræ mulieris vertebatur ornatum, nulla omit-
tens figmenta lasciviæ*—at night the Devil would
trick himself out like a beautiful woman and
forego no images of immodesty." The telling of
this occupies one line and a half, perhaps the
thousandth part of the biography.

Anchorites have sinned in their indiscriminate

condemnation of people who live in the World,
but the World has rendered back injustice for
injustice; it has ignored the poetry and exag-
gerated the fanaticism in their lives. Uncon-
sciously, perhaps, it is nettled by the silent reproach of every man or woman who forsakes it.

The life that St. Anthony led in exchange for
life in the World was upon this fashion. He got
his livelihood by the work of his hands, he
prayed, he strove "to make himself like one who
is conscious that he walks in the sight of God,
pure in heart, and ready to obey His will."
Though he wrestled daily with evil, there was
no harshness in him, nor lack of courtesy, but
sobriety of judgment and an equable spirit. The
fame of these qualities brought to his hermitage
a multitude who sought help in their various
needs. He consoled the sorrowful, taught the
ignorant, appeased the angry, and endeavored to
persuade them all to put nothing before the love
of Jesus Christ. "Seek ye wisdom, chastity, justice, virtue, watchfulness, care of the poor, robust
faith in Christ, hospitality, and a mind that over-
comes anger. If we observe these things, we shall
prepare for ourselves a mansion in the land of
them that attain peace." And for further information of his character, as it was trained and dis-

ciplined by his solitary life, I will quote from his
sermons: "The virtue that is within us needs no
help from without; for the native purity of the
soul, if it be not polluted by some external foul-
ness, is the source and origin of all the virtues.
It must be good, because a good Creator created
it. God has given us our souls in charge; let us
be faithful to the trust we have accepted. Do not,
I beg you, be frightened away by the word *virtue*,
as if it were impossible of achievement, nor think
the pursuit of it a sort of far pilgrimage; because,
under God's grace, it depends on our own will.
Let the Greeks [the unreligious] cross the seas
to other lands, that they may pursue their studies;
we need not travel, whether by land or water;
for in this and in every corner of the earth rests
a foundation on which to build up the kingdom
of heaven.

"Let Christians and monks have a care lest
their weakness give opportunity to the demons
of temptation. For according as these demons
find us and our thoughts, so are they wont to
make their way into our hearts. And if they find
there the seeds of fear and of an evil mind, like
robbers who take possession of undefended
places, they pile fear on fear and torture the
wretched soul. To conquer the enemy there is

[32]

one sufficient way, *lætitia spiritualis*—by the joy
of the spirit; and the thoughts within a soul that
is set upon God will drive them out, as we drive
out smoke. It is written, let not the sun go down
upon thy wrath; so let it be with every fault, let
not the sun by day, nor the moon by night, go
down witnessing it."

The drift of this reference to St. Anthony is
to show that from the very beginning of monasticism, complete separation from the world of
ordinary life does help a man to keep himself
from grossness and wrongdoing, and that, even
if he stay in his solitude, others will derive aid,
if it be merely from the inspiration of his victory,
whether they resort to him in the flesh or in the
spirit.

Athanasius goes on to say: "Who was there in
Anthony's company that did not transmute sorrow into joy, anger into peace? What blind man,
but felt the burden of blindness lightened? Who
that had been dejected by poverty, did not im-
mediately cast his dejection aside, despise riches
and even rejoice in penury? What weary monk
but was refreshed by his exhortations? What
youth, assailed by the temptations of the flesh,
did not after his counseling become a lover of
chastity? Who that had been perturbed by evil

thoughts, but left him, the storm within calmed
down and soul serene? For he comprehended the
griefs that beset each man, and by his own meritorious life had learned spiritual wisdom, and so
knew how to minister to their several ills as if
they had been bodily wounds."

Anthony (or at least Athanasius, or whoever
else has recounted the stories of his struggle with
sinful thoughts) conceived of temptations in the
most objective and concrete form. He or they
could not believe that a force so bent on evil, so
persistent, so protean, so subtle, could be other
than rational and living; and so, as the stories
passed from mouth to mouth among credulous
people ignorant of physical laws, the idea of a
horrible, personal Devil was created. But possibly
their exaggerations, primitive and gross as they
seem to us, are no worse, if we are to judge them
by their effect upon the lives of other men, than
the opposite habit of the World, which depre-
cates, excuses, diminishes, softening here, rubbing
out there, smoothing, and tricking out with par-
aphrase, gloss, apology, and special pleading,
until at last sin disappears like a puff of smoke,
dissolved in the unwholesome air of polite com-
plaisance. Of the two extremes, one is unlettered
and superstitious, the other flabby and brutal,

for it is only the brutes that are indifferent as to whether there is a right and a wrong.

I cite one more trait of this fugitive from the World: "His countenance had a great and extraordinary beauty in it. If any strangers wished for a sight of him, and found him in company with other monks, though they had never seen him they would pass by the rest and run to Anthony, as though drawn by his appearance. Not that he was taller or larger than others, but there was a peculiar composure of manner and purity of soul in him. For, being unruffled in spirit, all his outward expressions of feeling were also free from perturbation; so that the joy of his soul made his very face cheerful, and from the gestures of his body men understood the composure of his soul."

A fair inference from the biography of this early anchorite is that self-dependence in material things, and in religious things dependence upon what he called God, together with meditation, and prayer, and a tyrannical dominion over the fleshly appetites, do teach spiritual wisdom. And there can be no greater skepticism, no more certain indication of the working of the spirit that denies, than to suppose that spiritual wisdom in any man, however remote his life, or inaccessible his habitation, can be unfruitful for other men. And if devotion to such practices all one's life brings so many notable excellencies, may we not infer that partial devotion will confer some spiritual benefit upon the seeker?

VI
Saint Benedict

HE World's theory that anchorites do nothing for their fellow
men is contradicted by the life of
St. Anthony, and the similar reproach it casts upon monks is
still more flatly contradicted by the achievement
of St. Benedict. As Anthony is an archetype and
represents the anchorite's real relation to humanity, so St. Benedict is also an archetype, and the
growth and long prosperity of what he called *Do-
minici schola servitii*, his *School for the service of God*,
are proof of his usefulness to his fellows. And
since human nature remains a constant factor
throughout all the revolutions and mutations
that have come over our western world from
Benedict's day to our own, it is, as I have said,
no more than prudent for the neophyte, unless
he rejects wholly the notion that the past can
help the present, to examine a little into this
famous system.

The Benedictine rule is addressed to those
who yearn to enter into eternal life: *Quibus ad
vitam æternam amor incumbit.* And eternal life

does not mean a life hereafter; nor does it involve any reference to time, for time is but a condition under which mortal life is lived, perhaps a category or device of the human mind, and has no part in God. Rather, eternal life means the enjoyment of something that transcends all human limitations, the consciousness, if such be possible, of that which is perfect. In other words, the object of the rule is the knowledge and love of God. The method consists primarily in the practice of solitude; for solitude takes us away from worldly temptations, it affords opportunity for self-examination, meditation, and prayer, it quickens the desire for holiness, and brings us face to face with the mystery of eternal values. The practice of solitude is therefore an indispensable part of spiritual discipline. But solitude, if unregulated, in spite of its soothing touch, comparable to that of a child's hand, is unable of itself to give the recluse the peace that he most needs. Like unchartered freedom, solitude unregulated becomes a burden. Senancour, to take a modern instance, who fled from the maladjustments of the World, did not find in the life of a recluse the peace that he had hoped for; solitude with him begot restlessness and restlessness unhappiness. A recluse needs regularity of life, hours that bring their

appointed changes, definite tasks to do, whether
self-imposed or commanded by some outside
authority, otherwise disquiet will dog his steps.
This need is met by the provisions of the Benedictine rule; they serve as a trellis to support and
direct the shoots and tendrils of the religious imagination, they rescue untrained wills from tedious license and wayward reachings out to right
and left, and lift the spirit toward sunlight and
the upper air.

But ordinary human nature, even of a serious
cast, needs some indulgence on its quest of the
eternal values. Men, except such as are very
strenuous and tense, drawn like a bent bow to
the arrow's head, need some intercourse with
their fellows, especially with such as are upon a
like quest as themselves; otherwise they find the
long stretch of solitude, day after day, tedious
and unfruitful. Besides, company gives employment to the native kindliness in man; and the
union of many diminishes for each his servitude
to material cares, for by assigning to each the
duties that he can best perform; to one cooking,
to another the vegetable garden, to a third copy-
ing manuscripts, to a fourth illuminating missals,
and so on, the necessary tasks are more speedily
accomplished. Human fellowship, too, saves men

from whimsies and fantastical notions, to which solitaries are sometimes liable. And one monk may learn from another some virtue, some discipline, some practice, some thought or hope, some vision of the divine, which of himself he could not have discovered. And, also, in the offices of worship, in common supplication for fuller life and deeper spiritual satisfactions, there is a contagion that passes from man to man, so that if one man's heart is lifted up, his neighbor's heart is stirred and lifted likewise, as the first fledgling that spreads its wings encourages its fellows. For these reasons Benedict rejected complete solitude and gathered his monks together for the better attainment by all of their common end.

The several articles of the rule I need not recount. They prescribe obedience, work, prayer, and a strict observance of the *summa quies*, the perfect peacefulness, to which fugitives from the World aspire. They are addressed to those who are ready to renounce their own desires and become soldiers in the service of Christ. A brief enumeration of certain precepts, which, in the language of the rule, are instrumentalities of good works, will serve to indicate the spirit of the whole:—

Thou shalt love the Lord thy God with all thy heart, and with all thy soul, and with all thy mind, and ... Thou shalt love thy neighbour as thyself.
Thou shalt be a stranger to the World's doings.
Thou shalt not return evil for evil.
Thou shalt not love much talk.
Thou shalt be often on thy knees in prayer.
Thou shalt hate thine own self-will.

From this, in an imperfect way, one can infer the general nature of St. Benedict's monastic system. It was not, of course, intended to provide its members with a well-rounded life, nor to teach them the ways of men or a knowledge of this physical universe. Its purpose was to found schools for the service of God. Such a purpose stands over against the purpose of life in the World, and the opposition is justly expounded, I think, by Cardinal Newman. He ascribes to St. Benedict "for his discriminating badge, the element of poetry," and explains what he means by this as follows: "Poetry, I conceive, whatever be its metaphysical essence, or however various may be its kinds, is always the antagonist to *science*. As science makes progress in any subject matter, poetry recedes from it. The two cannot stand together; they belong respectively to

two modes of viewing things, which are contradictory of each other. Reason investigates, ana-
lyzes, numbers, weighs, measures, ascertains, lo-
cates the objects of its contemplation, and thus
gains a scientific knowledge of them. But as to
the poetical, very different is the frame of mind
which is necessary for its perception. It demands,
as its primary condition, that we should not put
ourselves above the objects in which it resides,
but at their feet; that we should feel them to be
above and beyond us, that we should look up to
them, and that, instead of fancying that we can
comprehend them, we should take for granted
that we are surrounded and comprehended by
them ourselves. It implies that we understand
them to be vast, immeasurable, impenetrable, in-
scrutable, mysterious, so that at best we are only
forming conjectures about them, not conclusions;
for the phenomena which they present admit of
many explanations, and we cannot know the true
one. Poetry does not address the reason, but the
imagination and the affections; it leads to admiration, enthusiasm, devotion, love. The vague, the
uncertain, the irregular, the sudden, are among
its attributes or sources."

Following this interpretation, the observance
of Benedict's monastic rule appears to be, in

part, a sort of meditative poetry, like much of
Wordsworth, and, in part, a passionate lyrical
hymn, such as those Latin hymns to be found in
the Roman Breviary, a poetry, however, not expressed in verse and stanza, in metre or rhyme,
but in quiet human lives. In Benedict's opinion,
the love of God is the spirit of poetry, and to
do His will is to become a poet.

VII

Thomas à Kempis

O qui scintillam haberet veræ caritatis,
profecto omnia terrena sentiret plena fore vanitatis.
Thomas à Kempis

AINT BENEDICT's foresight determined the form and usages of the system that was to serve as a house of refuge for fugitives from the World during all the Middle Ages and into modern times. The system was flexible and permitted different ideas or emotions to become predominant at one time or another, as work, asceticism, prayer, or contemplation. The reproach laid against it is that corruption donned cowl, cord, and sandals, and converted monasteries into abodes of idleness, if not worse. To which it may be answered, that the monastic system was never intended for all men; no monk, however enthusiastic, ever proposed that it should apply to everybody. As to corruption, that is a social problem, biological and psychological, whose solution concerns the World quite as much as it concerns the monastery. There is, of course, no magical remedy in a monastery to cure men of evil inclinations against their will.

The value of the monastic system is that it embodies ideas and practices which in the past have enabled serious-minded men to attain inward peace, and cultivate a knowledge and love of God. At any rate, the system endured in full fruition down to the Reformation and produced its ripest fruit shortly before the modern world determined, for one reason and another, to make an end of it. That ripest fruit is contained in Thomas à Kempis's book, *De Imitatione Christi*. Thomas's life was that of the typical monk; it contains no more incident than befitted the narrow monastery walls on Mount St. Agnes. To copy pious manuscripts, to fetch water from the well, to walk with patient feet up and down the little garden path while his thoughts soared far above, to hoe cabbages, to cook what food sufficed for his brethren and himself, to preach to novices, to compile biographies of saintly brothers who had gone before—such was his life.

With what sweet labour did your hands transcribe
The Word for those who shared your convent walls,
Brothers of Common Life,
Nor age, nor strife
Dimmed your swift vision of the Inner Word,
But with the clear-tongued message of a bird

Singing in April from an apple bough
You gave your gospel — as when sunlight falls
Piercingly into Shadow — Surely now
In the white-feathered host of Heaven you sing
The Song that was your earthly tutoring.

The Imitation of Christ is reckoned among the classics of literature, and takes its place beside the selected few of chiefest note, whoever makes the selection. It is the flower of monastic poetry. It sets forth the monastic ideal in its passion, its beauty, and all its imperfections. The imperfections are plain enough; that ideal detaches life not merely from the World, but also from all human affections and interests; it passes over the noblest human emotions, such as delight in beauty, the love of Dante for Beatrice, the passion of the mother for her son, and whatever other earthly feeling seems in the eyes of ordinary men to reveal most clearly a divine presence.

Such an outlook upon human life, such dogmas, are no longer acceptable, even to the recluse who has forsaken the World. But the book is immortal because of its passion, its truth, and its heroism. It is a noble exposition of one mode of spiritual life. It is based upon two postulates: that the World and its pleasures are vain things, and that the one way of escape lies in imitation of Christ; and it proceeds by a series of counsels, precepts, prayers, and praises, to instruct the novice how he may climb the long, steep road to freedom. The seeker must turn his back on temptation, practise humility, dwell upon religious thoughts, cleanse his soul by penitence and prayer, and, trampling upon all earthly desires, steadfastly follow in the footsteps of the Divine Leader, with a whole heart and unfaltering devotion. If we grant his two postulates, he is the wisest and most lovable of teachers. I quote here and there from his pages:—

Vanity of vanity, all is vanity, except to love God and serve Him only.

If you wish to stand erect and go forward in duty, you will deem yourself an exile and a pilgrim on this earth.

The beginning of all evil temptations is inconstancy of soul and little trust in God. As a ship without helm is driven hither and thither by the waves, so the weak man, losing hold of his purpose, is tempted on every side.

He that hath true love in no wise seeks his own good; his only desire is that the glory of God be shown forth in all things. He envies no man, for he is indifferent to his own pleasure; nor does he wish to enjoy himself, for above all joys he hopes to attain felicity in God.

He that purposes to commune with the inward things of the spirit must depart from the multitude, as Jesus did.

Leave vain things to the vain, and busy yourself with the commandments of God.

Strive to be patient and tolerate the faults of others and their infirmities, whatever they be; for you yourself have many which others must put up with. If you cannot make yourself such a one as you wish, how can you expect another to conform to what you approve of?

You know that you are come to be a servant, not a master, that you are called to labor and endure, not to sit at ease and talk.

By two wings a man is lifted up from earthly things, by simplicity and purity.

First establish yourself in peace, and then you shall be able to set others at peace.

He that shall best know how to suffer will have the greater peace, and he that is mistrustful of nothing shall be truly at peace.

Oh, if you would mark how much peace to yourself and joy to others you would procure by doing right, I think you would be more careful of your spiritual perfection.

If we were not wrapped up in ourselves, if instead we were dead to ourselves, then we should be able to perceive things divine, and experience contemplation of heaven; the whole hindrance, and it is very great, is this: that we are not free from passion and desire, nor do we strive to walk in the perfect way of the saints.

A man should so stablish himself in God, that he would not need much human consolation.

If you seek Jesus in all things, you will find him everywhere, but if you seek yourself, you will find yourself.

When you shall have come to this, that tribulation is sweet and savorous to you for Christ's sake, then believe that it is well with you, for you have found paradise on earth.

No man is fitted to understand heavenly things, unless he has stooped under burdens for Christ's sake.

Cardinal Gasquet says that "the monastic life adapts itself to the workings of grace in each individual soul, and gains its end when it has brought that individual soul to the highest perfection of which its natural and supernatural gifts render it capable." This assertion is true of Thomas à Kempis. His ideal strikes a chill into the heart of the ordinary man, who finds his pleasures at the family hearth, in the laughter of children, the welcomings of friends, the obvious achievements of prosperous labor, and the approbation of the community; but the monastic life is not for the ordinary man. The ideal of Thomas à Kempis is far different. He seeks by all means, great and small, to foster and increase his love of God; no duty is too menial, no renunciation too great, that enables his heart to burn with deeper devotion. And if one may venture to judge by the analogy of human affections, to love God, if that is possible, must be the highest human felicity.

VIII

Senancour, Eugénie de Guérin, and Amiel

Fili, quid hoc vel illud ad te? Tu Me sequere.
Thomas à Kempis

UCH then, in a general way, is the method by which solitaries of old sought to attain a higher life. Those of whom I have spoken constituted a part of the mighty theological and ecclesiastical system which guided and governed mediæval Europe, and for that reason it is popularly believed that both the salvation they sought and their way of seeking are inextricably bound up with that system, and must stand or fall with it. In order to avoid this objection to my argument from authority, I shall refer to sundry solitaries who were not, in any technical sense at least, members of that system. If it be again urged as an objection, that these also were religious-minded, I must admit they were; and if that quality shall debar a solitary from usefulness to-day, then I must admit, as a rule, solitaries will be useless. Almost all men who forsake the World become seekers of God, although the God they seek need not be the Christian God. But I deny that their religious-

[51]

mindedness is a bar to their usefulness, and I go
much further: I will rest my whole contention —
that solitaries serve the World — upon this very
quality of religious-mindedness, with the proviso
that they are not bigots but pilgrims in search
of what to them shall prove eternal life. My belief is that, as a rule, the modern solitary leaves
the World under the constraint of some tedium,
disgust, or sense of vanity, but that after he has
left the World he will be swept along, whether
by loneliness or some spiritual attraction, upon
a search for God; and yet perhaps it is that a
desire for God has aroused these several forms of
discontent. However that may be, I come to my
instances of hungry-hearted persons who do not
belong to the great monastic system, and yet have
sought salvation in solitude. Senancour found the
World to consist of "Embarras, ennuis, con-
traintes, insipidité." He says: "Pour moi, j'ai
appris avant tout, que le parti le plus sage serait
encore de renoncer à la vie du monde, si même
on n'avait rien de vraiment heureux à y substi-
tuer. . . . I no longer think of putting my life
to use, I only seek to fill it; I no longer wish to
enjoy it, merely to put up with it; I do not exact
virtue of it, rather that it shall do no wrong —
but even this, where may I procure it or even

hope for it? . . . Let us keep up our silent sanctuaries; in them the eternal perspectives are pre-
served, and such ideas as, at least to some extent,
restore a man to his moral composure, and serve
to rescue him from the degradation of the World.
. . . When the religious-minded has once beheld
beatitude in his visions he looks no more for
them on earth; and if he shall lose those ravish-
ing illusions he finds no charm in things far in-
ferior to his dreams."

To keep up our silent sanctuaries—that should
have been Senancour's task, as it was his duty.
But he achieved nothing because he wandered
about in search of a monastery built by human
hands out of bricks and clay, and did not learn
that each man must build a silent sanctuary for
himself out of spiritual materials, and that the
physical monastery is merely of value according
as it shall serve that end.

Eugénie de Guérin, on the contrary, — to come
to my second instance, — took the materials that
lay ready to her hands and built her silent spiritual sanctuary. And that spiritual sanctuary
seems to have converted her father's house into
its own essence, or at least into a corporeal counterpart. Simplicity was there, religious devout-
ness, pious practices, and a humdrum round of

daily duties. Her journal and letters contain little more reference to the outside world than do the records of Mount St. Agnes or of Sacro Speco. The early morning sun, the bird upon a bush outside her window, the chirp of grasshoppers, a brood of chickens, a lame duckling, the dog, the falling leaves, the fragrance of flowers, these constitute the furnishings of life. Her spirit is like that of Thomas à Kempis. She says of a friend: "I have noticed Gabrielle does not approve my inclination to retirement and renouncement of the World. She does not know me; she is younger and does not understand that a time comes when the heart lets go of all that does not help it to live. The World enchants and intoxicates, but that is not life. Life can be found only in God and in oneself. To be alone with God, oh, happiness supreme!" And in another passage: "I have not read the life of the saint for the day, I am going to read it; I always do before dinner. I find that while one is eating, it is good to have in the soul something spiritual like the life of a saint. The Life of St. Macédone is charming. He is the saint that said to a hunter, who was amazed to meet him in the mountains, 'You run after beasts, but I run after God.' These words contain all the life of saints, and also of men of the World." She

[54]

calls herself *pauvre anachorète*, and with reason;
and writes to her brother, "What would *you* do
with my perpetual calm? For, except for what
comes from my heart or from my head, there is
no movement in my life. At this moment I have
just come back from a little walk in the sunshine;
there was nothing stirring near me except some
flies buzzing in the warm air. I was alone in the
great empty monastery. This complete loneliness
made me live for an hour as hermits have lived
for years, men and women, souls withdrawn apart
from the world. Without material cares, with no
word but from within, with no emotions but those
that start within the mind, with no life but that
of the soul: there is in this unattachment a freedom full of enjoyment, an unsuspected happiness, and I well understand how, in order to make
it last, one would go and hide a hundred leagues
in the desert. . . . It is because the world does
not satisfy the soul; it entertains it but does not
give it life. One feels this, however young, when
once the heart detaches itself from illusions."

And with her, as with St. Benedict, the spirit
of poetry was a familiar visitant. "I write," she
says, "with fresh hands, for I have just been
washing my gown in the brook. It is pleasant to
be washing, to see the fish pass by, and ripples,

blades of grass, leaves, or flowers fallen in — to watch these, and I don't know what beside, float down the stream. Many things come to the washerwoman who has eyes to see the brook as it goes by. It is the birds' bathroom, the sky's looking-glass, the image of life, a running road, the reservoir that fills the baptismal font." And so, for good reasons, she was content. "Rien ne me plaît comme mon désert."

My third instance is Amiel. Thomas à Kempis says: *Pacem omnes desiderant; sed quæ ad veram pacem pertinent, non omnes curant. Pax mea, cum humilibus et mansuetis corde. Pax tua erit in multa patientia.* These words almost seem like the summing up of Amiel's journal. His soul was that of a recluse, but circumstances did not permit him to flee from the World, and it may be that he did not know that solitude would be for him not merely a road, but the only road, to the peace he sought, to freedom from the burden of trivial things. He seems to have understood himself no further than to have been aware that he was too sensitive, too imaginative, too self-distrustful, for practical life. He yearned for what Wordsworth describes : —

Senancour, Eugénie de Guérin, and Amiel

> What but this,
> The universal instinct of repose,
> The longing for confirmed tranquillity,
> Inward and outward; humble, yet sublime:—
> The life where hope and memory are as one;
> Earth quiet and unchanged; the human Soul
> Consistent in self-rule; and heaven revealed
> To meditation in that quietness!

Amiel beats his wings against the constraining walls builded about him by society. "Vivre de la vie éternelle, c'est là le but et la félicité suprême pour le philosophe, l'artiste, le saint. Eh bien, vivons de la vie éternelle. . . . Il n'y a de repos pour l'esprit que dans l'absolu, pour le sentiment que dans l'infini, pour l'âme que dans le divin. . . . Il n'y a qu'une chose nécessaire: posséder Dieu."

> La vie est une lutte et dès lors un supplice,
> Et c'est là sa laideur, et c'est là mon effroi.
> L'harmonie et la paix sont mes désirs à moi,
> C'est pourquoi vers ton gouffre, ô saint Bouddha, je glisse.

Is it not the stirrings of a yearning for God that arouse this angry swarm of discontents?

IX
The Influence of Christian Tradition

Qui autem Te per contemptum mundanorum, et carnis mortifica//
tionem sequuntur, vere sapientes esse cognoscuntur: quia de
vanitate ad veritatem, de carne ad spiritum transferuntur.
Thomas à Kempis

OLITARIES, as I have said, either before they leave the World, or after they have left it, become religious-minded, and it is true that their religious-mindedness is likely to be colored by the Christian doctrines which the World has so long professed. Certainly not only Eugénie de Guérin but also Senancour and Amiel were deeply affected by them. Those Christian doctrines sanction and approve the idea and practice of the monastic system—manual and intellectual labor of certain limited kinds, prayer, spiritual exercises, and meditation. The modern solitary who, we may suppose, has wandered far from sectarian dogmas, is apt to prick up his ears at this sanction. He scents superstition. He is fearful lest Christianity should prove to be much more than sponsor, that if there had been no Christian Church, there would have been no monastic practices, no discipline of solitude, no prayer, no spiritual exercises, no meditation, but that all such ideas and doings would have been relegated long ago to the limbo of outworn superstitions. He is afraid that though Christianity may lay claim to poetry and visions beautiful, yet the World holds fast to common sense and truth, and that for the sake of his intellectual integrity he must not take up with ideas and practices that spring from error.

Let us give this apprehension due weight. It must be admitted that the Christian Church has moulded our civilization and our ways of thought, and still maintains dominion over our sentiments, and through them affects our judgment. She plays a great part in matters that touch our dearest emotions. She enters as a solemn visitant into the great ceremonies of life and death, she has inherited much of the noblest achievements in art, her cathedrals are the most glorious buildings on earth, her steeples and belfries add a charm to the loveliest landscapes that embrace human habitations, and on Sundays and feast days she displays her power and authority in every city, town, village, and hamlet. The position of Christ in theological thought is proof of her amazing hold on educated men. Many a philosopher still professes her dogmas, and her traditions exert a profound influence

[59]

Pro Uita Monastica

upon us all. It is very difficult for earnest-
minded men who yearn after things of the spirit
to approach any problem of spiritual life quite
free from the ideas taught by the Church. If that
theological and ecclesiastical system invented the
road that leads away from the World and devised those practices which St. Benedict counseled as right occupations for the employment
of solitude, then the pilgrim should undoubt-
edly pause and consider. Nevertheless, it often
happens that one road serves men who travel
from very different motives: one traveler may
take the high road to London for the sake of
pleasure, another for business, and yet it will
lead a third to worship at Westminster Abbey.

The Church may be wrong in her dogmas,
wrong in her interpretation of the solution of
the deepest problem in life, notwithstanding,—
and herein lie her strength and her justification,
—she poses that problem correctly. She has taken
to heart the saying of her Lord, that man cannot
live by bread alone; she perceives that human
weakness reaches out its hand, that man craves
a satisfaction which the senses cannot yield: she
recognizes his aspiration toward knowledge of religious truth, his yearning for a Divine Friend,
his hunger for Infinite Love. Such phraseology

[60]

as this may not be acceptable to the pilgrim, but put into other words it means nothing else than that, for some persons at least, a man's salvation lies in turning toward a knowledge of that which shall best satisfy his craving for knowledge, and toward a love that shall best satisfy his craving for love. And the pilgrim himself cannot formulate his problem otherwise than as a consciousness of a driving need for intellectual and emotional satisfaction.

The Christian system fared badly when the World laid hands upon it; men of the World, servants of ambition or pleasure or compromise, added, altered, painted, and rearranged, put tinsel on and gaudy trimmings, and covered up the simple outline of the first design. But when these trappings and amplifications are pulled off, the formula of human needs reappears in its native simplicity. These needs are inherent in human nature. To these Christianity added hope, and the Church added dogma. So long as the pilgrim follows the road taken by these religious needs, inherent in the heart of man, he should not be troubled merely because Christian hope and ecclesiastical dogma are companions of his way.

Grant that infinite multiplicity is assumed to be a unity because of the nature of the human mind or because of the tendency of philosophic thought to simplification; grant that God is identified with Jesus Christ because of our inability to deal with metaphysical problems, of our practical human need that Godhead be expressed in terms intelligible to men of all kinds and classes; grant that the Holy Ghost depends upon the assumption that our human craving for holiness implies an objective reality; grant that the Church is the corporate expression of human need for a royal road by which common men may travel toward that which for them is the highest; grant to skepticism the justice of all its doubts, grant to those who deny the Christian creed the truth of all their denials; nevertheless, you but show the more plainly the two elementary religious needs of the human heart, knowledge and love. These remain in spite of doubt and denial, the data for the gravest human problem.

X

Some Grounds of Doubt

These our actors, as I foretold you, were all spirits.
The Tempest

F, however, the pilgrim is still afraid that he may be sinning against his intellectual integrity, that the World may be right in asserting that men should stick to prose, should take the universe as the senses reveal it, should enjoy life all they can, not drop the bone for the shadow, like the dog in the fable, let him reflect for a little upon the nature of that certainty which seems to the World so firm and solid. A very brief consideration will raise doubts, and incline him to suspect that poetry may hold as much truth as there is in prose, or possibly more.

I accept (let us suppose) my subjective self; I am a spectator that perceives; but what is it that I perceive? A long stream of pageantry forever shifting, flowing onward like a river, the present scene passing rapidly beyond the horizon of consciousness, and a new succession of imagery coming into its place, and yet never a glimpse of the machinery, if there be such, that shifts the scenes. So it is from birth to death, from dark to dark, a

stream of pageantry and nothing more. If we draw
the inference that there must be some reality to
cause these shifting pictures — vibrations of ether
to cause our perception of light, vibrations of air
to create sounds, and other manifestations of energy to stir other sets of nerves to action, nevertheless, across the chasm that divides outer vibrations from the pictures in consciousness there
is no bridge of explanation. And besides, the
nerves respond to but some of the vibrations that
buzz in the outer world; so that even if it were
possible to get outside of consciousness and have
knowledge of vibrations as they really are, our
knowledge of that outer world would be but frag-
mentary and therefore necessarily misleading.
And further, even if the neural shocks that reach
the brain were truth-bearing messages that could
be interpreted by an impartial mind, they meet
no such interpreter; for the mind has been so
moulded and twisted by past experiences that the
original message is quite distorted in its interpretation, the meaning gets translated into a lot
of ready-made, happy-go-lucky sentences. Every
perception is tricked out, as it were, in the tailor
shop of memory and the millinery parlors of
imagination, and never reaches consciousness in
its native state. And if we consider the eternal

[64]

sequences of movements, causes and effects, how can we be sure that this effect, or that, necessarily follows upon a cause? Or, if we turn our attention to what we call nature's laws, what indubitable warrant have we to believe, for instance, that there is conservation of energy, when no experiment in its same circumstances can ever be repeated? How can we feel confidence in any information whatever concerning outward reality?

And if we pass from the stuff of life to its pattern, the World has still less justification to demand our acceptance of its views. To be sure, in this particular it can hardly be said to possess a theory of its own, since the doctrine of "Let us eat, drink, and be merry" ignores all questions of why, whence, and whither; nevertheless, when the World—if it ever bothers its head at all about the matter—takes over from science the hypothesis of irrational forces, it fares no better, for science has no theory upon metaphysical causes and ends. Science merely propounds a series of activities, which quite without purpose have constituted this sensitive instrument, consciousness, and then play upon it, *adagio* or *allegro*, a sequence of random notes. Such an hypothesis seems fantastic, almost whimsical, as an explanation of the pattern of life.

But suppose the novice insists upon credulity, and wishes to believe that the perceptions report external reality as it actually is; how can he? If he examines his mind, he finds it primarily an organ to secure the preservation of his life. Its natural propensities are to fix its attention on food and drink, sleep, danger, and escape. Animals with intellectual aptitudes for metaphysical truth could never have survived. The mind is an instrument, like another, shaped and adapted for its primary uses. If reality in all its endless variety passes before it, the mind will perceive and grasp only what may serve its body's interests. And even if it have avocations, and lay hold of aspects of reality that do not concern the primary instincts, what warrant is there that it does so from a love of truth? And supposing the mind be obsessed by a love of truth, what hope is there that it grasps even a thousandth part of that multitudinous reality? If a reader were to read only every tenth word of a book, what would he know of its contents?

And if a man, before he puts his trust in what we call knowledge, must postulate the truthfulness of perceptions, he must do as much for memories, since perceptions, without the support and interpretation of memories, are meaningless.

But reflection shows how capricious memory is. Of a hundred thousand perceptions only a bare scattering are remembered; and these all by favor. Here, too, the body's interests are paramount. M. Bergson says that one function of the mind is to forget, to discharge itself of the myriad superfluous perceptions that our senses pile upon us.

And there is a further difficulty about memory. What proof is there, apart from convenience to philosophy, that to-day's memory is a true counterpart of yesterday's perception? To be sure, the image in memory asserts its own truthfulness, but what evidence can it adduce? Yesterday's perception is gone, never to return; we cannot recapture it, set it and its memory side by side, and compare the two. And what reason is there to suppose that memory is more veracious than perception? And yet perception is a notorious false witness, for as we know, it flatly asserts the objective existence of color, solidity, substance, and science denies all this.

However, let credulity have its way, and not only accept the truthfulness of perceptions and of memories, but also assume that memory preserves what is pertinent and necessary to a true comprehension of reality; even with this raw

[67]

material all secure, in order to decipher and comprehend the meaning of that material, the novice must have recourse to reason. All our perceptions and memories are sifted, sorted, arranged, placed in sequences and figures, by reason; for it is not the rude chaos of perceptions and memories that of itself is supposed to reveal reality, but the rearrangement by reason. And how can we put confidence in reason? Look at its origin in order to judge of its authority. We find that, in the course of life upon this globe, reason is comparatively a newcomer. In the biological scale, long before we go back to our unicellular ancestors, there are no traces of human reason to be found, no laws of thought in operation, no power to feel the cogency of *hence* and *therefore*. The origins of life lie far back of the beginnings of reason, in a "dark backward and abysm" of elementary stimuli and reactions. What warrant have we, then, for a belief that reason, born of things without reason, can and does arrange our perceptions and memories in accordance with the pattern of objective things that exist outside of mind?

Difficulty treads on the heels of difficulty. If reason may be trusted, nevertheless its processes and conclusions must be expressed in words, and

Some Grounds of Doubt

words are full of prejudices, inheritors of old par-
tisanships, most fitful in their elusive and subtle
metamorphoses. And suppose that we vault over
these obstacles, we find from observation that in
practice we pay little regard to reason. Many another guide exercises quite as much control over
our beliefs as reason does. Authority, for instance,
or fashion. The routine of daily life, our food, our
customs, our schools, churches, courts of law, our
tastes, our admirations, obey authority or fashion.
In all the great interests of life, as the potter's
wheel shapes the vessel of clay, so imitation, not
reason, shapes our conduct. And, looking further
afield, human life appears to be very impatient
of reason, eager to get rid of it as a troublesome
accessory. That part of the business of corporeal
life best carried on, such as breathing, digestion,
the circulation of the blood, is quite free from the
interference of reason. Bodily acts that follow
mechanically upon stimuli are our best; next in
merit come instinctive actions. Consider what
would happen, if in a moment of imminent danger action should pause while reason was debat-
ing whether life is, or is not, worth the living. In
the scale of biological merit, next to instinctive
action comes habitual action, such as reading,
writing, walking, eating, which have properly

[69]

been taken from reason and handed over to habit. Wherever life has been able to shove reason aside, it has done so.

Surely a pilgrim need not stick to the prose of common sense, nor fear lest faith and imagination shall lead him astray. Faith and imagination are the two distinguishing traits of mind, the two factors of knowledge, the two primal conditions of human existence; without them the senses and reason would be the very shadow of vanity. Why, then, should the pilgrim distrust them when they busy themselves with religious matters?

XI
The Bounties of Solitude

I long for scenes where man has never trod —
 For scenes where woman never smiled or wept —
There to abide with my Creator, God,
 And sleep as I in childhood sweetly slept,
Full of high thoughts, unborn.
John Clare

AN it be that the World is right
to lay its stakes on physical fact as
against an ideal philosophy? How,
for instance, can Dante's vision
beautiful, that *Donna beata e bella*,
that Florentine maiden so endowed and informed
with heavenly communion that she is become all
immortal and divine, be explained as superfluous
imagery in consciousness, sketched at hazard by
the blind hand of physical fact, busy with its physical task, as if charred sticks wheeled on a barrow
by a careless laborer might rub against the wall
he passes by and trace the outline of Signorelli's
angels? The choice before the pilgrim seems to
lie in finding the cause of the gorgeous imagery
in Dante's mind, either in the blind mêlée of
physical energies, unknown except as causes of
such imagery, or in the magnetic force of some
final end toward which struggling, thwarted, spir-

itual instincts pursue their course "as birds their trackless way." Is he to believe in chaos or teleology, in Nature or God?

Long ago Pascal said: "Voilà ce que je vois et ce qui me trouble. Je regarde de toutes parts, et ne vois partout qu'obscurité. La nature ne m'offre rien qui ne soit matière de doute et d'inquiétude. Si je n'y voyais rien qui marquât une Divinité, je me déterminerais à n'en rien croire. Si je voyais partout les marques d'un Créateur, je reposerais en paix dans la foi. Mais, voyant trop pour nier, et trop peu pour m'assurer, je suis dans un état à plaindre, et où j'ai souhaité cent fois que, si un Dieu la soutient, elle le marquât sans équivoque; et que, si les marques qu'elle en donne sont trompeuses, elle les supprimât tout à fait; qu'elle dît tout ou rien, afin que je visse quel parti je dois suivre. Au lieu qu'en l'état où je suis, ignorant ce que je suis et ce que je dois faire, je ne connais ni ma condition, ni mon devoir. Mon cœur tend tout entier à connaître où est le vrai bien, pour le suivre."

Who wins the wager? where does reality lie? Dean Inge says: "One test is infallible: whatever view of reality deepens our sense of the tremendous issues of life in the world wherein we move is *for us* nearer the truth than any view

which diminishes that sense." Surely our pilgrim
need not fear wronging his intellectual integrity
because he turns his back upon the World's material philosophy as well as on the World, nor
because, upon his path away therefrom to solitude, he consorts with men of a religious mind,
nor even with persons steeped in Christian beliefs. Many another, not a Christian, seeks out
solitude and its religious inspirations. To show
that our pilgrim need not be fearful, I quote from
a solitary quite free from theological and ecclesiastical traditions.

" Ah! I need solitude. I have come forth to this
hill at sunset to see the forms of the mountains
on the horizon — to behold and commune with
something grander than man. Their mere dis-
tance and unprofanedness is an infinite encouragement. It is with infinite yearning and aspiration that I seek solitude, more and more resolved
and strong. . . .
" I thrive best on solitude. If I have had a
companion only one day in a week, unless it were
one or two I could name, I find that the value of
the week to me has been seemingly affected. It
dissipates my day, and often it takes me another
week to get over it. . . .

Pro Vita Monastica

"There is nothing so sanative, so poetic, as a walk in the woods and fields even now, when I meet none abroad for pleasure. Nothing so inspires me and excites such serene and profitable thought. The objects are elevating. In the street and in society I am almost invariably cheap and dissipated, my life is unspeakably mean. But alone in distant woods or fields, in unpretending sprout-lands or pastures tracked by rabbits, even in a bleak and, to most, cheerless day, like this, when a villager would be thinking of his inn, I come to myself, I once more feel myself grandly related, and that cold and solitude are friends of mine. I suppose that this value, in my case, is equivalent to what others get by church-going and prayer. . . . It is as if I always met in those places some grand, serene, immortal, infinitely encouraging, though invisible companion, and walked with him. This is a common experience in my traveling. I plod along, thinking what a miserable world this is and what miserable fellows we that inhabit it, wondering what it is tempts men to live in it; but anon I leave the towns behind and am lost in some boundless heath, and life becomes gradually more tolerable, if not even glorious. . . . Solitude was sweet to me as a flower. . . . I love to be alone. I never

found the companion that was so companionable
as solitude."

But in addition to the reproach of outworn religious beliefs, critics of the recluse often charge
that solitude involves mental emptiness and idleness. Not at all. There is no more reason to suppose that a solitary is empty-headed and idle
than that men of the World are empty-headed
and idle. Undistraught by the society of men, the
solitary may turn his attention to other creatures
and created things; he substitutes new interests
for old; he has leisure to look about him at this
curious universe and turn over some of its pages.
There are all the stars of the sky, "the Pleiades,
the late-setting Boötes, the Bear, which men also
call the Wain, that circles round in its place and
gazes at Orion," just as they were when Odysseus
set his course by them and steered his raft from
Calypso's isle to the land of the Phæacians. There
is the earth with all its elements and energies, its
records of ancient times, of physical mutations
and geological contortions, where the recluse
may sit upon the ground and read sad stories
of dead nations, species extinct, and epochs
barely decipherable. He may make acquaintance
with humble fellow travelers from birth to death,

horses, dogs, sheep, cats,—they are but other manifestations of the wayward spirit of life, for the breath they breathe is one with ours,—the shy squirrel that may by patience be coaxed to accept morsels from the solitary's lunch, the bees busily bringing pollen from stamens near at hand to pistils far away, all unwitting (as we with our odd conceptions of knowledge assume) that they are creating fresh sources of nectar and ambrosial meal for the next generation of bees.

There are the wild flowers in all their modesty and glory: the blueweed that covers barren fields with a benediction of violet hue, such as Fra Angelico chooses for the saints in Paradise; the joe-pye weed that might supply color for Persian painters painting a sultan's palace in Persepolis; the staminate early meadow-rue that shakes its drooping stamens like golden bells at a fairy wedding; the yellow melilot that might grow in a poet's dreams; and pendulous bellworts that hang their heads under the burden of their Latin polysyllables. The World cares little for roadsides, upland pastures, swamps, or stony fields; it prefers Broadway, the Boulevard Haussmann, Piccadilly. The solitary does not wish to divert the World from its haunts and bring it to his solitude—by no means; why, then, should not

the World let the solitary alone, or even gently
encourage him in his retired ways, instead of calling him a slacker and a do-nothing?

But the ultimate justification of solitude lies
in its function as a nurse to the religious spirit.
Many a man finds there, and there only, what
Wordsworth refers to as the sense "of something
far more deeply interfused," and which old Seneca
calls "the presence of some god." An effluence
emanates from Nature, as if the great mother, in
the closer communion and deeper sympathy of
solitude, folded her arms about her children and
hummed old tunes which she had heard before
the birth of worlds.

In solitude the recluse has leisure to ponder
over the most significant fact in life: that there
are values. I do not mean the difference of rank
in the organic scale of creation, but the judgment of "better" or "worse" that the perceiv-
ing mind passes upon all images that excite its
interest. It seems as if that high judicial faculty
dealt with the inmost verity in life. And in solitude, far better than in company, the recluse may
brood, during what time he likes, over speculation as to whither this verity may lead us.

XII
The Vegetable Patch

Seek and ye shall find.
St. Matthew, vii: 7

ISCONTENT with false values is the motive that has impelled all monks and recluses, from St. Anthony to Thoreau, to leave the World. Solitude, I repeat, best can furnish the recluse with the conditions under which he may hope to readjust those values until they shall, at last, rest on the foundation of complete mental satisfaction. In solitude the monks of old attained that goal. If we go on a quest, all agree that it is prudent to start with an hypothesis; and the most reasonable hypothesis must be based on the experience of other seekers, who believe that they have found. Why should we be deterred because they expressed the satisfaction of attainment in an outworn theological and ecclesiastical language? Has Cicero nothing to say to us because he wrote in Latin, or Homer because he wrote in Greek? Those monastic seekers thought that they had come upon reality, and they called it God; and in the acceptance of values based upon that reality they

[78]

found peace. Modern seekers are doubtful if
men's minds can lay hold of reality; and yet it
is difficult to suppose that he who has attained
to perfect peace can be persuaded that he has
not touched reality at least with his finger-tips.
Some modern philosophers declare their belief
in a Reality, all-embracing, of which finite creatures, each in its several way, are finite expressions.

The recluses of old withdrew from among the
congregations of men and built a monastery
out of wood and stone, bricks and mortar, on a
remote mountain-side, or in some clear valley
where they should hear the waters of a river
hurrying to find peace in the great sea, *quel mare
al qual tutto si move*. A monastery, as its name
shows, is primarily a place where one lives alone,
or, at least, a place for the practice of solitude.
Absolute separation from all men is virtually impossible, and that is not what the recluse seeks.
His need is merely separation from what he calls
the World. And according to traditional usage
a monastery provides not only solitude but also
modes of employment. Of these modes four are
preëminent—garden, library, oratory, and cell.
This system is still a wise guide; the recluse in
his retreat cannot do better than to follow it.

The letter killeth, but the spirit giveth life. The mediæval world is past, its social institutions are gone, the feudal system will never return, nor will the great monastic orders ever lift their heads again. But as graftings from a wild stock may be brought into the orchard, and seeds from mountain flowers be planted in a garden bed, so it is possible to bring from the long past ideas that once clothed themselves in antique or mediæval forms and will now take modern shapes and add richness and variety to our modern ways of doing and thinking. Even the feudal system may stimulate our imagination. In feudal times, social inequality — men rising one above another in place and dignity, of diverse education and diverse occupations, groups and classes varying in duties and privileges, with different modes and conditions of living — presented the spectacle of a society in which men looked up without envy or malice, and even found life richer from the thought that there were degrees of excellency and honor, and imagined that it was a privilege to serve and work for somebody better than oneself. But most men prefer a level plain to the mountains; they can build railroads, drive motor cars, trucks, and lorries more expeditiously in the flat country, build cities more

easily, and accumulate wealth far more speedily.
And yet some men had rather be poor moun-
taineers and live in highlands, surrounded by
peaks and mountains that lift their tops toward
heaven, than to be rich burgesses dwelling in the
plains. In like manner the bygone monastic system offers ideas and suggestions to us of to-day.
Let me avail myself of it as an allegory: for as we
still go to the Bible to find the deepest religious
experience of mankind, so in the monastic system we shall find recorded a great part of whatever success men have achieved in their search
for spiritual wisdom. Much of the allegory must
be taken as such, but other parts may be accepted
literally or interpreted as if parables, according
to the need and condition of the reader.

Let the recluse, then, begin his period of iso-
lation and self-discipline in a garden, and at first,
following the Benedictine regulation of labor in
return for livelihood, let him go to work in the
vegetable patch. It is not necessary that this
monastic garden be shut in by walls, like its
European predecessors in mediæval centuries;
let us suppose it to lie far out in the open country, with the bay of some great lake, or estuary
of the sea, spreading out its curve of blue at the
foot of the monastic precincts. A mountain range

bounds the horizon to the north, and a shelter-
ing fringe of spruce and hemlock hedges the
garden in. Even the neighboring hamlet in-
trudes on the monastic seclusion no further than
to send up faint columns of smoke from busy
kitchens, nor the outlying farms, apart from cheerful barnyard noises, nor the farmer except when
he sings or whistles as he drives his plough. The
recluse lays out a corner of the garden for potatoes. He looks into the future, and sees, in his
mind's eye, rows of plants full grown, laden with
leaves and flowers, and down within the little
mounds of earth, clusters of tubers firm and fresh.
This vision he hopes to bring to birth in the
world of tangible things, and he sets out to co-
ordinate the forces of nature in such manner that
the potato patch shall come to be a copy of his
thought. Other hands, perhaps, in the summer
before, digged the soil deep; and during the win-
ter Jack Frost has been grinding the particles of
earth finer and finer, so that our solitary steps in
after the process of preparation has commenced.
He takes a spade, digs a trench north by south,
six inches deep, another two feet away, and another, until the patch assigned to potatoes is all
taken up; he then lays along the bottom of each
trench some stimulating fertilizer — an admixture

of wood ashes, lime, dead leaves, together with
manure from the barnyard—and over that he
scatters a thin covering of earth. These strange
bedfellows prepare the ground for the infant life
of the plant, nurse the tender sprout, warm and
comfort it, and enable it to lift its haulm out of the
dark into the air and sunlight. Having prepared
the bed, the recluse must take parent potatoes,
carve them into segments, cutting out in prefer-
ence the eyes from the apex, and lay the sets,
eyes upward, along the bottom of the trench
(carefully, lest they touch the manure and the
flavor of the future potato be impaired), and then
cover them with earth. And when he has done
this and laid aside the spade, he will take up the
hoe, since he must uproot the weeds; for though
Nature will help him grow potatoes, yet she is
the universal mother, and in her passionate, wayward fashion, loves all her children—weeds, as
they are despitefully called by lovers of domes-
ticated flowers, quite as much as vegetables or
flowers themselves. Then from hoe back to spade,
to bank the earth about the sprouting plants; for
although stalk, leaves, and flowers should have
all the sun that shines, the tubers, often much
against their will, must stay well covered up in
the dark. And day by day, through all the grow-

ing season, the recluse must watch the plants, and guard them jealously from insect and disease; he must mix fungicide, take pump, and spray and spray.

When his back feels broken, then he may pause to lean upon his spade and muse over the process. First, clear and distinct in his mind's eye, gleamed the idea, and this idea with a sort of kingly authority summoned him to work; it roused desire, desire stirred will, and will in some mysterious way despatched currents down the motor nerves; and hands, arms, legs, hurried to combine materials and forces that should give corporeal substance to his original idea. Man, sunshine, rain, manure, the minerals in the soil, all toil together in patient collaboration to help the little underground stems lay up their stores of starch. The recluse now perceives that he is an agent in creation, bringing order out of chaos, laying a yoke on the neck of the untamed actual and breaking it into the service of the ideal. But not quite that, for these powers are as ready and eager as he; they are not slaves, but colaborers. In the *idea* lies power; out of the *idea* flows forth energy. This is one of the first lessons taught under the monastic system.

[84]

XIII
The Flower Garden

Mid Nature's old felicities.
Wordsworth

Heureux celui . . .
Qui plane sur la vie et comprend sans effort
Le langage des fleurs et des choses muettes!
Baudelaire

HE vegetable patch of a monastery does not ask of its gardener more than such parts of his time as may be strictly necessary for the crop, since the monastic rule recognizes that flowers are as necessary for the spirit as food is for the body. A solitary in quest of values that shall rest upon the ultimate satisfactions of the soul must go by way of a flower garden.

Giovanni Baptista of Ferrara, full of a noble confidence that the flowery path will lead to heaven, bids one tread *floridam ad cœlum viam*. And a lay brother of the Carthusian Order, for thirty years gardener to the Charter House in Paris, says: "The culture of gardens has always been looked upon as the fine art of the world: nothing can afford more pleasure than the pursuit of it. This is the pleasure I wish to a curious

[85]

person, who disengaged from the tumultuous scene of the world, and inspired with a sense of religion, has taken up a resolution to pass the rest of his days at his country-house, where he may taste the innocent pleasures of a rural life."

Consider, for instance, the Canterbury Bell, *Campanula Medium.* If it is not a poet's flower, like daffodils, pansies, roses, or rue, that must be because its name will not fit into English verse, for surely it is a most enchanting and romantic flower. Bells speak a language of their own to the human heart. No wonder that the Church as prologue to its liturgy introduced the ringing of the bell. A bell of metal cast by the masters at Bruges is an exquisite achievement of art and science. The fused metals obey their foreordained ratio; every circle and curve in their molten union, from crown to mouth, has been prescribed by primal laws that rule the waves of sound. And when the sun sinks below the horizon, the novice leans his hoe against the wheelbarrow and listens in the direction of the parish church till a rope is pulled, the bell swings, and the heavy clapper strikes the rim, and notes of solemn music fly through the air and in devout processional glide across the waters of the bay. *Ave Maria!* Involuntarily he repeats such verses as may start up in his memory:

Vergine, s' a mercede
Miseria estrema dell' umane cose
Giammai ti volse, al mio prego t' inchina;
Soccorri alla mia guerra;
Bench' i' sia terra, e tu del ciel regina.

But the music of the Canterbury Bell is still more melodious and devout. For my part, I think, especially when it wears its true color, blue or white, that it should be called Campanula Virginis, except that the Campanula is far older than Christianity. She was a nymph. As the story is told, her father was a fantastic youth who always went about tinkling a bell, and her mother "a subterraneous nymph," and, so long as the daughter lived, their happiness was without parallel. Campanula was vigilant and faithful; and the Hesperides, mistresses of the wonderful garden, gave her an office of trust in it, which was that whenever a thief came to steal the golden apples, she should arouse the guardian dragon. Campanula flung herself in the way of every thief, and at his touch she uttered a tinkling sound that warned the dragon. But one night a robber murdered her. The Hesperides, in order to comfort the stricken parents, transmuted her body into a flower and planted the flower in their garden, and gave orders that it should be carefully

tended. And Sieur Liger d'Auxerre, who tells
the story, says "fidelity is a virtue that always
recommends a man, not only during life, but
even after Destiny has lodged him in his grave."

The Campanula Virginis is very beautiful; and
what a miracle! A little seed, a little soil, a little
water, and the glorious sun, and down go little
roots into the earth, the green stalk lifts its head,
its tender leaves uncurl, and at the top of every
stem a bud starts forth, unfolds its corolla, and
becomes a bell. Do the upholders of a mecha-
nistic universe go into their laboratory and produce an achievement like this? The psychologists, however, tell us that the pleasure we get
from the Campanula Virginis is due not to the
sensations of light, color, line, and shape, but to
an accompanying affection, which should not
be confounded with the sensations themselves;
nevertheless, they do not tell us what *raison d'être*
that accompanying affection may claim. How and
why did this sense of beauty come? Out of what
was it evolved, or what power fashioned it?

Flowers make one of the monastic textbooks,
and the lesson that St. Benedict the poet would
have the solitary learn is the lesson of beauty.
For those that are not trained psychologists it
is not an easy lesson. What biological end does

the love of beauty serve? If the recluse shall,
day by day, as the sun climbs the same arc of
heaven, watch the light glide softly along the
outer convexity of the corolla till it reach the
lip, then creep within and gild the pistil with a
deeper yellow, and shift the hues of green upon
its leaves, does he make himself more fit to out-
live his less sensitive competitors? Are lovers of
beauty survivors in the struggle for life? Does
nature select them as a favorable variation? It is
sometimes said that delight in beauty plays a rôle
in the drama of sex; but what planted in the
feminine mind the love of beauty? Delight in
beauty, if it shall explain the victorious wooing
of the beautiful lover, must have arisen first.

In the monastery beauty teaches other dogmas and another goal, another theory of fitness.
Can it be that beauty, of which men talk so much,
is a mere accident? Is the spiritual exhilaration
engendered of loveliness in nature and art of no
advantage in the life of men? Are all the artists
that have ever lived wholly wrong? Let an artist
build, write, compose, paint, or model, yet, though
his work should last for a thousand years, though
he should receive a great price, though his name
should become a household word, if he knows
that there is no beauty in his handiwork it is a

failure in his eyes, one vanity the more. Is beauty really empty of all meaning? Art, perhaps, may achieve its purpose in human appreciation, in the pleasure of the moment derived from the work of art. But Nature differs from Art. Nature brings forth nothing that is an end in itself; whatever she does is for the sake of that which shall come after, and that, too, is for the sake of its successors. "In sequent toil all forwards do contend."

May it be that we have erred by assigning to the power which acts through Nature a mere material, a mere physico-chemical, task? The theory in the monastery, at least, is that beauty serves some ultimate end, is some masterful manifestation of reality, or, as the old phraseology expressed it, a shadowing forth of the divine. The solitary is taught that the flower should give him some such satisfaction as comes to a traveler who has lost his way in the forest, when he catches sight of a blazed tree and learns therefrom the direction that shall guide him toward his journey's destination.

XIV
The Library

In sortem ac libertatem transiens filiorum Dei, qui stant
super præsentia et speculantur æterna.

Thomas à Kempis

HE second discipline of a retreat is the library. The novice might expect to find upon the shelves books of theology and devout learning, lives of saints, treatises upon ethics and such, and little else. He would be wrong. The monastery imposes no such limitations; rather it encourages, if it does not oblige, its inmates to read widely in any or all regions of this printed world, wandering whither they will. Some special literature or topic is advised. On first quitting the World there is likelihood that the recluse is too much under the influence of grief, cynicism, or scorn, and the best way to wash his mind of these impurities and restore it to a state of serenity is to steep himself in far-off things. Take Greek literature, for example. One need be no scholar in order to stumble about and grope one's way in Homer, in Plato, or Euripides, and thereby forget oneself. The strangeness of this Greek language, with its sup-

[91]

pleness and sinewy elegance, holds the recluse; and the Hellenic world in all its richness and nobility, its surrender to passion and its love of form, is the best of medicines. In that intenser world of old the modern reader cools his own heat of grief or disgust. Here is diversion in its best sense. Behold Achilles, swift of foot, and godlike in his strength and youthful beauty, mightiest of warriors, standing by his tent in sullen rage at the dishonor put upon him by Agamemnon. In his absence from the battle, the Trojans have burst their way over the protecting wall, across the ditch, and are setting fire to the Grecian ships. His dear friend, Patroclus, runs up with the news, weeping; and great Achilles says:—

> Why dost thou weep, Patroclus, like a foolish
> Little girl, who running to her mother asks
> To be taken up, tugs at her gown and pulls
> Her back as she walks on, and cries, and
> Looks with longing, till she be taken up.
> Thou art like her, Patroclus, weeping these tender tears.

Does not the scene make us forget ourselves? Or take the most famous trial in history, where Socrates defends himself by alleging that he has followed what he believed to be the divine command: "Verily, this is so, ye men of Athens.

Wherever a man shall take his place in the battlefield, whether he thinks that to be the best place, or has been ordered there by the commander, there — as I think — he should stay, and abide danger, and not deem death or anything else worse than shame." And he tells his judges that, should they offer to spare him on condition that he shall refrain from his former ways, he will answer: "Ye men of Athens, I entertain high regard and affection for you, but I shall obey the god rather than you; and so long as I live, and am able, I shall not give up philosophy, nor my exhortation, nor stop expounding my belief to any one of you that I may meet, saying in my customary fashion, 'My dear fellow, are not you, an Athenian, a very great city and of high renown for wisdom and power, ashamed to busy yourself about money, striving to get as much as you can, and about reputation and honors, and not busy yourself nor take thought of wisdom, and truth, and of your soul?' . . . For I do nothing else but go about trying to persuade you, both young and old, not to busy yourselves about your bodies or about money more than about your soul — how it may become very noble; and I say that virtue does not come from money, but that from virtue comes money and all other

[93]

good things, whether to the individual or to the
state. . . . Therefore, I say, O Athenians, acquit
me or do not acquit me, for I shall not do dif-
ferently, not even if I have to die many times."
There, before the recluse, as he reads the immortal pages, Socrates pronounces his apology,
in the presence of the three accusers, while to the
east stands the acropolis crowned by the Parthe-
non, and beyond rise the outlines of Pentelicus
and Hymettus, and to the west shimmers the
sea, and out of the blue waters Salamis lifts her
memorable head; and there, quivering with reverence and admiration, in among the blind-eyed
judges, for the moment, stands the recluse also,
oblivious of the two thousand five hundred years
between.

Or if he be troubled by the sin-wrought woe
in our modern world, let him read *The Trojan
Women* — how Hecuba goes from the ruins of
high prosperity to slavery.

Fiction, too, is part of the discipline. Here
the recluse, as it were, returns to the World
again but with a difference. We are so used to
this world of fiction that it appears as natural,
as much a matter of course, as the physical
world of ordinary life; and we are apt to forget
that, as a rule, a novel is for a man to read by

himself and not in company, that it is a sort of
handmaiden to solitude. This is a world, so far
as the life of civilized man is concerned, as ample,
as populous, as dramatic, as full of vicissitudes, as
the world of sensuous experience. The palaces
of Shakespeare, Cervantes, Goethe, Walter Scott,
the mansions of Tolstoi, Balzac, Victor Hugo,
Thackeray, and Dickens, the summer parlors
of Stevenson, Hawthorne, Motte-Fouqué, Fo-
gazzaro, all lie open, unobstructed by bolt or
bar. In these places of delight and joy, of fear
and terror, the recluse wanders about at will,
unseen, unheard. In the midst of the stir and
bustle of life he preserves his solitude. And the
reason that the monastic discipline enjoins such
reading is that at the beginning of his novitiate
there is danger lest the recluse be too much absorbed in repentance, self-reproach, regret, and
downheartedness; not at once can he attain the
source of strength that he seeks. Besides, he
must not let his heart lose the one good gift the
World occasions — its quicker beating for compassion, pity, admiration, or scorn. In the world
of fiction he beholds Desdemona, Cordelia, Mar-
guerite, the heroines of Turgueniev or George
Eliot, and untrammeled by consciousness of self,
embarrassment, shyness, incapacity, unembit-

tered by any personal wrong from the doers of evil, he gives himself up to the flood of sympathy.

And in this world of fiction the recluse observes that there is both good and evil, intermingling, bound together, now one predominant, now the other, but neither visible in the utter absence of the other, twins, each dependent for existence on its fellow. And yet, in spite of the eternal presence of evil, no reader blames the author. Nobody is indignant with Shakespeare for Lady Macbeth, Iago, Regan, Goneril, or thinks that he did wrong to create them. Wickedness is part of the texture of the whole, the shadow against which the light shows most triumphant. And further, although he praises most those dramas or romances in which there is no trace of the master's hand, but each character is left to fashion its own salvation or destruction, nevertheless, if he be a real lover of books, he will value most those in which, as he imagines, he can discern a personality, not in this act or that, not in this character or that episode, but rather in a quality comparable in subtility to the ethereal element that fills the interstellar spaces — of which the lover of books is mysteriously conscious, as of the memory of something fragrant in a forgotten dream.

Most of all, the world of fiction, being a world of ideas, teaches the recluse that in order to make a world there is no need to postulate ponderable matter or shocks of energy; that consciousness is the ultimate element; and that ideas constitute the reality that enters into human experience.

The Spiritual Power of Sex

Donna è gentil nel ciel.
Inferno, ii, 94

HE quest for new values, the search for a well of water drinking wherefrom one shall not thirst again, is, according to the World, a wild and foolish chase, and it is certainly so far wild and indeterminate that it is much more prudent for the seeker to adhere to tradition and the trodden path. Many others have sought; and the road of tradition is the summing up and conclusion of all their experiments. This road, as I have said, led men from the World, whether for life or for a season, into a retreat where they meditated upon spiritual forces and the various modes of the revelation of God. In these meditations some were stirred to reverence and belief by the story of the New Testament; others by the beauty, the tenderness, the grandeur of nature, the song of birds, the expanse of ocean, the daffodils that outdare the swallows, the rathe primrose; and others by the miracle of human love. Animals breed; gross appetite is all that Nature needs to induce obe-

dience to her great law, "Be fruitful and multi-
ply"; then why should she superfluously squan-
der chemical energy merely to produce a passion more a hindrance than a help, that would
renounce all appetites and self in an ecstasy of
metaphysical imaginings? Why should mere animal union bear such an emphasis? —

> I love thee with the breath,
> Smiles, tears, of all my life! — and, if God choose,
> I shall but love thee better after death, —

why, unless the end of life be to attain some
higher spiritual existence, to mount on the wings
of mystery nearer to God, or to serve Him by
helping bring some nobler world to birth? However much, during periods of retreat, men came
to find God in the New Testament, or in nature
roundabout, still they longed for an ampler, a
more intimate, revelation; and, lo! by the inter-
vention of grace induced by their striving after
holiness, the scales dropped from their eyes and
they perceived that here in common life is the
very revelation that they sought; yet how full
of perplexity, mystery, and evanescence. The
animal, man, stands in the presence of a miracle. By the consecrating magic of spiritual love
the divine is revealed in the human, and, while

that passion glows, remains visible; but when the spiritual fire dies away, the vision vanishes. Whence did the revelation come, and whither did it go?

Upon such speculations men in retreat are wont to ponder; and in the early days of Christianity, before science had done and undone all it has, a result of that pondering was to apply the talisman of sex to spiritual uses, and personify the divine revealed in woman. Materials lay ready to hand. According to the story, a Jewish maiden was betrothed to a carpenter. Her firstborn son went forth to preach his doctrine that the Kingdom of God is within us. In the brief biographies that tell his life she appears but momentarily here and there, and — except at the annunciation — in the background. She keeps his childish sayings in her heart, as all mothers treasure up the sayings of their first-born sons; she goes to look for him when lost; she waits upon the outskirts of the crowd while he is preaching; and when he is crucified she stands hard by the cross. A scant half page would more than hold her history, and yet the words concerning her have been like the mustard seed in the parable. Human needs laid hold of her. Christ, abstracted by an arid theology, had as-

cended to the highest heaven, to act as Judge
on the *Dies Iræ*, leaving behind him an austere
image which masters in mosaic have depicted on
choir vaults at Venice and Monreale. The spec-
ulative intelligence required an explanation of
the spiritual love of man for woman; sinners
needed a new mediator; men, sensitive to the
finer influences of sex, needed a mother, needed
a maiden, needed the sympathy and love man
cannot give to man. And at last the image of the
Virgin Mary arose, crowned with light. By her
maidenhood she touched the sentiment of chiv-
alry in man, by her motherhood she entered
every human heart. Her conception was im-
maculate, and therefore, the natural passing into
the supernatural, this creature, born of spiritual
desire, grew to become the tenderest, the most
compassionate, the most humanly necessary
emanation from the godhead. Down from heaven
and Deity she came, maiden and mother, to earth
and men. From the sculptors of Rheims and the
glass-stainers of Chartres to Memling and Fra
Angelico, from the jongleur of Notre-Dame to
Dante and Petrarch, throughout all Christen-
dom, in the old world and the new, the Virgin
visited and blessed her worshipers with a love
equaling the love of living women. Deity of itself

cannot know sorrow; but Mary had learned on earth the greatest lesson of sorrow.

Stabat mater dolorosa
Juxta crucem lacrymosa,
Dum pendebat filius;
Cujus animam gementem,
Contristantem ac dolentem
Pertransivit gladius.

Sorrow teaches compassion, and compassion bestows the final grace on motherhood. So schooled and disciplined, Mary became to men what Michelangelo expressed in his *Pietà* and Dante in the last canto of the *Paradiso*. Unnumbered thousands have prayed many a prayer like that of St. François de Sales: "Ayez mémoire et souvenance, très douce Vierge, que vous êtes ma Mère et que je suis votre enfant, que vous êtes très puissante et que je suis un pauvre petit être vil et faible. Je vous supplie, ma très douce Mère, que vous me gouverniez et défendriez dans toutes mes voies et actions." Little can Deity do for men if it cannot play the mother's part. And, of old, in the scheme of things, this was possible; good men and sinners stretched forth their arms and heard her voice upon the inward ear, beheld her radiance with the inward eye, felt her pres-

ence shed round about, like the coolness of a
summer's evening, such as falls on close-clipped
lawns and graveled walks bordered by lilies and
the flowering plum. The sun's white light is too
puissant for mortal eyes; it must be veiled in
clouds, or visit first the opaque, corporeal world,
and only then, refracted and diminished, may it
come unharmful, in a thousand colors and hues,
to fall upon the tender retina. In like manner,
Deity would be unbearable if revealed direct, so
it is shrouded in infinity, veiled by human doubts
and human ignorance, and only shines upon the
dull souls of men in a refracted and diminished
way, through instrumentalities that poets call
visitants from heaven but men call children,
wives, or mothers, or dawns on the imaginative
mind in the gracious image of the Virgin Mary,
or in the idea of Christ. But the Virgin's image
and Christ's divinity have been rejected of men,
and cast aside, and Deity is again shrouded in
impenetrable clouds.

XVI
The Realm of Truth

THE recluse paces the cloister, impatient with iconoclasm, however useful or necessary iconoclasm may be, since any child or barbarian can pull down; he is interested in building up a spiritual edifice in which his soul may dwell and be at home. He marks the magical power in an idea: how it may burst the coverings in which it is encased, may germinate and grow, may draw in life and nourishment from human needs, or rather, how human needs are able to seize upon the tiny seeds of hope, tend and watch over them, warm them with desire and water them with tears, breathe into them the faculty of growth, and at last create a divine power that in its turn, inspired by gratitude, will bless and prosper its creators and servants. It was after such manner that the hermits, the saints, and the sinners of the Middle Ages recognized, or created, the gracious image of Our Lady—for creation is nothing else than by apprehension of the mind to separate and give intelligible form to circumambient forces, which unapprehended,

[104]

undifferentiated, unformed, would remain mere manifestations of chaos. In this way the rational mind obtains the uniformity of nature, the phenomena of causality, and perhaps time, or even space. The wondrous and strange part is that whenever the soul of the external universe is apprehended or moulded by the spiritual needs of man into some spiritual form, it reveals itself as a helper. Reality lies neither in repetition, nor duration, nor the concordant testimony of multitudes of men; it is a manifestation of power, and must be measured by its effect in human experience. For the solitary the reality, *la vraie vérité*, exacts reverence and demands worship; and yet, if this be so, reality must exist somewhere; and where can that abiding-place be? It is not in matter; it is not in mere perceptions, confined within the human mind. Neither the flux of motion within the circumscription of space, nor the thinking mirror on which momentary images are flashed, can be more than a place of transitory visitation for the august spirit of reality.

Our Solitary, so meditating, recalls to mind what Plato, the poet, thought. There is a region far above the perturbation of life, the waywardness of desire, and the dominion of the senses: a realm of ideas, of universals, as philosophers

call them, pure, everlasting, immortal, change-
less. These ideas are the archetype of what, to
men occupied with the satisfaction of earthly desires and appetites, passes for reality. To them
these pure spiritual realities are abstractions from
the concrete, fictions of thought, names for the
traits and qualities of things, convenient symbols in practical reckonings. " Universals are not
real," they say ; and in so saying make use of the
very realities they deny. For in order to make
this denial, they must invoke the idea of reality,
the idea of being, and the idea of ideas; and
the three are universals. Indeed, neither speech
nor thought can do without them. We recognize
something because it embodies an *idea* that we
know; or if we recognize a thing because of its
similarity or relation to another thing, that is
because the similarity or relation is an *idea* that
we know. Our faculty of thought depends upon
this "pure, everlasting, immortal" realm, of
which a distinguished philosopher says: "It is
unchangeable, rigid, exact, delightful to the
mathematician, the logician, the builder of metaphysical systems, and all who love perfection
more than life." It is, indeed, the home of perfection ; there dwell Wisdom, Fortitude, Sobriety,
and Justice; there dwell the attributes of Deity.

But the quoted phrase suggests too marked a contrast between life and perfection. The two spheres are separate, not contrasted, for in life there is always endeavor after perfection, as creeping babies try to stand and walk; and though life never attains, it aims persistently at the goal. Here and there some laborious disciple of Justice, Truth, or Beauty seeks to embody his vision of that ideal, shining far off in its incorruptible heaven, within the visible, the palpable, the near at hand. Or rather, should we not say that from among the crowd of unilluminated, every now and again Justice, Truth, or Beauty selects one man or another to be her servant, entrusts her thyrsus to his hand, and bids him do her will in the material world?

Meditating upon Plato, the Solitary advances toward the chapel. Beside the door, within the wall is a recess, and in the recess an image of the Virgin. He pauses again: —

> Donna, se' tanto grande e tanto vali,
>   che, qual vuol grazia ed a te non ricorre,
>   sua disianza vuol volar senz' ali.
> La tua benignità non pur soccorre
>   a chi domanda, ma molte fïate
>   liberamente al domandar precorre.

Lady, so great art thou, so great thy power,
  That whoso wishes grace, and seeks thee not,
  His longing wishes, without wings, to fly.
Thy beneficence not only succoureth
  Him that doth ask, but many times
  Of its own will anticipates the asking.

Does this little image in the recess depict nothing
more than fancy? Is not Our Lady real? In the
pure region of ideas two are conspicuous, maidenhood and motherhood. To the Solitary it appears
as if, in the greater days of creation, when spiritual life first appeared on earth, each of these en-
nobling ideas was detached, differentiated, separated, from the general mass of ideal chaos, and
given its specific aspect by some spiritual faculty
(for so he is wont to term faculties that minister to the soul's needs), as vibrations of sound
are differentiated from vibratory chaos by the
nerves within the ear. Just as, to compare spiritual things with material, a sculptor cuts out his
statue from the enveloping block. An idea of
beauty lies within the cliffside of Carrara waiting
for the eye of genius to discover it; why should not
an idea of beauty lie unseen within the mass of
the ideal, until it is separated and given shape and
name by mortal needs? Does matter cease to be
everlasting because it wears the corporeal form of

Hermes, or idea lose aught of its immortal essence because it takes a woman's shape? We are
wont to say that in moments of inspiration the
mind creates beauty and discovers truth. We
might say equally well, the mind discovers beauty
and creates truth. Phrase it as we please, there is
some faculty within men which, in moments of
high passion, fine frenzy, or holy resolve, creates
love, heroism, or the works of genius. Some such
faculty finds its material in the realm of ideas.
That realm is truth; and when some spiritual
Prometheus fetched down the idea of motherhood and the idea of maidenhood, the primal
essence of truth still remained in them.

And how did they come together, making one
out of two? Is their union a sort of marriage
that incorporates and makes them one, or is it a
unity of double aspect, existent from all eternity?
But however it came about, there, in that immortal realm which the poet-seer Plato beheld, the
realm "dear to those who love perfection more
than life," the two gracious ideas met. Tentative
meetings there had been long before Plato's
time, such, for instance, as that of Demeter and
Kore, Mother and Maid, but because Demeter
and Kore were not pure universals the attempt
failed. Under the wiser direction of Christian

needs the two joined in absolute union to create
the beneficent concept known on earth as Our
Lady. This combination may be likened to a
chemical union of two substances which require
also the action of a third to enable them to drop
their individuality and become one substance.

However, the manner and time of the birth of
Our Lady as a divine idea is of no consequence;
the beginnings of things (whether the start of individual life, the origin of protoplasm, or the first
appearance of mind) are vague, undetermined,
and, for those who judge of values by what shall
be, rather than by what has been, quite irrelevant. The needs of mankind discovered, or oc-
casioned, or, if one may choose to put it so,
wrought the miracle, just as they discovered, oc-
casioned, or wrought the ideas of Beauty, Justice, and Truth. These needs, as metaphysicians
might say, joined together two universals and
a particular. The particular is the Mary of the
gospels. But historic fact, having served its purpose as a dissolvent of the separateness of the
component ideas, hung so light and loose about
Our Lady, that she was able to drop that element, to let it melt, evaporate, and disappear,
leaving only pure, immortal idea behind. This
new *idea* is a pure universal: witness its copies

here below—Notre-Dame de Paris, de Rheims,
de Chartres, de Lourdes, Our Lady of Westminster, of Durham, Die Jungfrau of Aachen or
Munich, la Madonna di Siena, di Firenze, del
Carmine, Mater Dolorosa, Mater Amabilis, and
thousands more.

Our Lady—and to each lover she presents an
individual aspect—lives in the abode of ideas,
and her power, like all other manifestations of
power, depends upon the relation between her
and her worshiper; she will influence his life according to his sensitiveness and his ability, just
as a love of Justice or a passion for Beauty may
move a man to do acts of justice or embody an
image of beauty. No force can produce an effect
unless the object it works upon is sensitive to
its push and incidence. The reason for denying
to her the possession of reality seems to be
that when men began to become more and more
interested in material things, more and more
steeped in the cares and pleasures of this world,
then her image grew faint, and her power also,
and that, when all interest in her departed, then
she, too, as if she had been but the shadow of
faith, vanished altogether. So might we think
that light is unreal when we cease to see it because there is no object present to intercept and

reflect it; or that our neighbor, who goes aboard a ship and sails away, has passed into nothingness; or that some art of color in glass or contour in pottery has been annihilated because it has been forgotten. And, we may ask, what would this seeming solid be, which we call the earth, this evoker of sensations, this object of speculations, what would become of it, if mind should perish? Is it more permanent, more real, more true, than an idea? And if we anticipate that time when this fair earth shall have become cold and dry, all verdure gone, the glorious oceans, circling round the globe, hardly to be traced in deeps and hollows, and all thinking things departed, and with them all memory, all capacity for thought departed too — shall Beauty and Justice and Truth likewise perish? By no means. In their pure, immortal, everlasting, unchangeable realm they will continue as before, eternal and uncorrupted, ready to inspire the heart of any new-born thinking creature that may come to life with a passion to reproduce once more fair copies of ideal things in the visible and the tangible. And if humanity shall reappear with sex, with mother and children, Our Lady also will be there, with her Child in her arms, eternal in her maidenhood, eternal in her motherhood, with the love light in her eye, and the smile on her lips, gracious in her divine assurance that purity is a gleam from on high, and that a child is the revelation of God. Surely she will be there to bless any thinking thing in human form. She may, in her remote loneliness, have lost the memory of the Hebrew maiden and have forgotten that her name is Mary; but new creatures in human form will kneel, in conscious or unconscious prayer, to the eternal ideas of maidenhood and motherhood, and again picture them in the most beautiful of human images.

Or, if this gracious image shares with speech and thought our human powerlessness to express any aspect of truth, and proves but one more ill-chosen symbol, still man must not weary in his endeavor to consecrate the power of sex to spiritual uses; for if it be humanly possible to believe in a revelation of God, our best hope lies in the sanctification of this mysterious duality. In the realm of truth all is possible. Who does not, at least in his blessed moments, hear in his heart the song of the Mystical Chorus?

> Alles Vergängliche
> Ist nur ein Gleichniss;
> Das Unzulängliche
> Hier wird's Ereigniss;

[113]

Pro Vita Monastica

Das Unbeschreibliche,
Hier ist es gethan;
Das Ewig-Weibliche
Zieht uns hinan.

All that is corruptible is but a symbol; that
which on earth is unattainable takes corporeal
form in this realm of Truth; and what is beyond language there steps forth a fact; the Holy
Spirit that manifests itself in woman lifts man to
Reality.

XVII
Self-Examination

Ego sum lux mundi: qui sequitur me non ambulat in tenebris,
sed habebit lumen vitæ.

St. John, viii: 12

S our Solitary constitutes the con-
gregation of his monastery, the
hour of vespers depends upon
his mood. His meditations have
aroused a restlessness which urges
him forth. He slips back the bolt of the great
gate and walks out of the cloistered precincts,
across the neighboring fields, through pastures
where browsing cows begin to turn their heads
homeward, and up a footpath into the woods,
with a purpose to reach the hilltop and win a
prospect of the setting sun. The shadows fall
longer and longer, and the cool of twilight sends
emissaries before. Once he is well in the woods,
the little voices of flora and fauna, heedless of
his presence, chatter round about him. Leaves
rustle, boughs creak, frogs sing, the white-
throated sparrow pipes its melancholy dactyls,
and crows caw clamorously. But more clear and
definite than these exterior sounds, he hears a
voice. There is no one on the mountainside but

[115]

himself, and the voice is obviously the articulation of his own thoughts; nevertheless, so near does it sound that he involuntarily pauses and looks about for the speaker.

Voice: Why do you try to deceive yourself? Why do you play at an imaginary game?

The Solitary stops to think; his only wish is to answer truthfully, but it is so hard to catch the shifting turns of thought and put them into words. The absurd similes that come into his mind annoy him, — Æneas clasping Creusa, Achilles unable to overtake the tortoise, chase of a greased pig, — but their very mockery of his attempt to catch his thought seems to furnish him with an excuse.

Solitary: I try to think the truth; but truth is hard to think.

Voice: Every one can say what he believes.

Solitary: No; the man who can say definitely what he believes is not thinking. Belief concerning the deep things of life is a living thing; and every element in it is forever shifting; a presentment of it as fixed and static is necessarily false. If a man is able to define his creed in rigid articles, it is because all his feelings have been cast into prepared categories, and his recital will read like the advertisements of an auctioneer. His tenets will be abstracts, condensations, epitomes, generalizations. Belief is motion, a breathing, palpitating, living thing; but an articulate creed consists of frozen slices of thought, real or fancied, ready for display in a front window.

Voice: You seek excuses. I am not asking for delicate discriminations of thought. Your creed remains in substance the same from day to day, living though it be, just as your body retains its identity, although that changes too. Give over your evasions and fencings.

Solitary: I will try.

Voice: You profess to reject the teachings of common sense; but it is your moral unwillingness to face facts that seeks refuge in skepticism. Some minds, perhaps, find it possible to disbelieve in the assertions of common sense; but are you, if put upon your honor, one of them? Your living, your daily routine, your every act is an acceptance of its doctrines. Even your professed skepticism of reason itself is the result of a chain of reasoning. Answer me truthfully. Do you not really accept this common-sense, matter-of-fact, physical world that your senses report?

Solitary: I do not. Nothing is more sure than that there is no evidence of any common property shared by a material world and the mental interpretations of it.

Voice: Well, if you object to the word *material*, call it an ideal world, mental stuff, the substance of consciousness, the mind of God, or whatever you choose; my question is, Do you not accept a fundamental distinction between images, or ideas, or feelings, that we may call sensuous, and the imagery of a dream or of your imagination — a distinction which in common speech we designate by the adjectives *real* and *imaginary?*

Solitary: I cannot tell. It may be that my difficulty lies here, similar to that which I expressed in regard to the formulation of a creed. I usually think of your common-sense world as being a world that science can deal with, that is, as static, cut up into forms and shapes by the processes of perception and memory, whereas I believe reality is a continuous flux, which, quicker than you can say of it, "This is so," is something else. The distinction you postulate as a test of reality has no meaning for me. My test is quite other than that. To my mind all thoughts, ideas, feelings, or dreams are equally real, and the one important difference between them lies in the degree of value that they severally possess for me.

Voice: But you do acknowledge an uncontrollable quality about the actual present that makes it of a different kind from the pictures of your imagination, and different, too, from the imagery in your memory?

Solitary: How can I tell? If uncontrollability is a proof of reality, all the images in dreams or delirium are certainly real. If my will appears to control the images in my imagination, what warrant have I that my will is not as uncontrollable by me as your physical reality? And then I shall have at one remove the same evidence of their reality that you rely upon for proof of the existence of a material world.

Voice: But the physical world persists, and reappears each time you turn to it.

Solitary: Persistence and repetition are no proofs at all; for if one appearance of an image has no element of reality, ten thousand repetitions will not corroborate it.

Voice: Remember that by your skepticism you are not raising your phantasies to the level of reality, but dissolving reality into a world of dreams.

Solitary: I admit a difference between what you call perceptions and what you call ideas; only I do not concede that this is a difference of reality.

Voice: All I ask is for you honestly to recognize that the difference is fundamental—the difference, let us say, between the Beatrice Portinari who married Messer Simone de' Bardi and the Beatrice of the Divine Comedy.

Solitary: I do.

Voice: Then, to take a further instance, Our Lady is a whimsy of your imagination, and it is childish to pretend that she has any power of any kind other than that which she receives from your fancy.

Solitary: My fancy did not create her. I found her. She manifests herself to different men under different forms. Her manifestation to me is the most real of my experiences. She ministers to my needs. She comes with me upon my walks. She kneels beside me at my prayers. I see with inward eyes her smile; with inward ears I hear her voice; her counsels, her advocacy, her teachings do not vary with my moods. What she is, I cannot say, but real with some kind of existence.

Voice: Then all the fancies of lunatics are real.

SELF-EXAMINATION

Self-Examination

Solitary: Oh! You drive me round and round this eternal circle: perceptions, memories, fancies. A perception is as real as the thing perceived; a memory is as real as a perception; a fancy in the imagination is real, too, furnished with powers and influences of greater authority than any reality which does not affect the mind.

Voice: You are trying to create gods, as the heathen do, out of any materials that lie ready to your hand.

Solitary: You are the Spirit that denies, and life is one eternal affirmation.

The Solitary paused; no voice answered. He listened, but heard nothing but the rustle of leaves, and the murmurous hum of insects. To his surprise he suddenly became conscious that he was walking at high speed, and that his body was all in a perspiration. He reached an open field on the crest of the hill, stopped, and looked about. The church bell in the far village was ringing the Angelus. The sun had sunk behind the darkening mass of the western mountains, but the bay still flushed with the thrill of color as it faded away. The blue of heaven deepened, rising higher and higher, as it seemed, into the farthest re-

cesses of space, and also descending nearer and
nearer. Soon the long shadow of the mountain
rim clasped the whole landscape in its embrace,
except for one fair field upon a hillside across the
bay, which still shone bright as the last lingering
rays of the setting sun kissed it good-night. The
Solitary murmured, involuntarily: "The Lord
is in his holy temple, let the whole earth keep
silence before him." He smiled to himself, and
stood for a time bareheaded. His feelings shook
themselves free from body and bodily sense. It
seemed as if his individual existence had lost itself in an innumerable crowd of other existences,
all striving, with one accord, to chant the same
litany — as once, he remembered, he had joined
in the Hallelujah Chorus in Carnegie Hall. He
looked up at the stars, and shivered with a sudden cold, of terror tempered by defiance, at their
inhuman immensity; he shouted, Hallelujah!
and with a warm gush of gratitude for the kindly
earth and the presence of familiar things, he hurried homeward.

XLIII

The Oratory

My house shall be called the house of prayer.
St. Matthew, xxi: 13

ANY people experience little quickening of the spirit in a church. They prefer to worship —if that word will cover a state of mind unexpressed in outward acts—in "a building of God, an house not made with hands," or, as Carlyle says, "in the great temple of Eternity," or in woods, or along the shore of ocean, since to the devout, trees and waves are fellow worshipers. But most seekers find comfort, a sense of far-reaching fellowship, a help for the concentration of thought, a ladder for contemplation to climb up by and to forget that by which it climbed, in the pious instruments devised by men to express their sentiments, for worship and praise—a church, printed words of prayer, the chords of Palestrina, or pictured saints in marble and fresco. In a church the seeker feels that he is in high communion; the spot has been sanctified by tears and sobs, repentance, agony, and holy vows, by hopes of rising up from falls, of amendment

[123]

and victory, of belief in the presence of God and of rejoicing angels. In a retreat, therefore, it is the custom to go to some church or chapel to pray.

One such oratory I remember. It was constructed after the old Romanesque manner, and very small. A few candles burned before the altar. At the back, on the concave ceiling of the little apse, the Byzantine image of God the Son looked down in imperial severity. The tarnished gold of the enamel flickered with the flickering of the candles. A faint smell of incense filled the little space, and a tenuous vapor imparted a vague mystery to the altar, the outline of the windows, and the barrel-vaulted ceiling which, were a man to stand on a bench, he could touch with outstretched hand. All was dim, unintellectual, irrational, mystical, mediæval. Is there not here, I thought, some likeness to the soul, struggling upward, in the little, candlelit, house of bodily life, with no better symbols of spiritual life than smoky images? A worshiper was there. He knelt down and read prayers from his breviary by the poor light of the candles:—

Sicut enim non est a carne sed super carnem, quod carnem facit vivere: Sic non est ab homine, sed super

[124]

hominem, quod hominem facit beate vivere. Quocirca ut vita carnis anima est, ita beata vita hominis Deus est.

For, as that which giveth life to the flesh is not from the flesh but above the flesh, so that which giveth spiritual life to man is not from man, but above man. Wherefore, as the life of the flesh is the soul, so the spiritual life of man is God.

Miserere Domine!

Late have I loved Thee, O Thou Eternal Truth and Goodness! late have I sought Thee, my Father! But Thou didst seek me, and when Thou shinedst forth upon me, then I knew Thee and learned to love Thee. I thank Thee, O my Light, that Thou didst thus shine upon me; that Thou didst teach my soul what Thou wouldst be to me, and didst incline thy face in pity upon me. Thou, Lord, hast become my Hope, my Comfort, my Strength, my All.

Miserere Domine!

Almighty God, Father of mercies, be pleased to work in me what Thou hast commanded should be in me. Give me, O Lord, the grace of an earnest sorrow.

Miserere Domine!

[125]

By thy holy love and fear, keep me from sins
of temper and of the tongue.
Miserere Domine!

O Lord, my God, Light of those that see, and
strength of the strong; hearken unto my soul,
and hear it crying out of the depths.
Miserere Domine!

O donna in cui la mia speranza vige,
  e che soffristi per la mia salute
  in Inferno lasciar le tue vestige;

.   .   .   .

Tu m'hai di servo tratto a libertate
  per tutte quelle vie, per tutti i modi,
  che di ciò fare avéi la potestate.
La tua magnificenza in me custodi
  sì, che l'anima mia, che fatta hai sana,
  piacente a te dal corpo si disnodi.

O Lady, in whom my hope finds strength,
  Who for my soul's health did endure
  In Hell to leave thy footprints;

.   .   .   .

Thou from my slavish state to liberty
  Hast drawn me up, by all the paths, by all
  The ways that thou hadst power to do;

Let thy high majesty keep watch on me,
So that my spirit, which thou hast made whole,
Dear in thy sight, may shuffle off this clay.
Miserere Domine!

Tout l'univers est plein de sa magnificence:
Qu'on adore ce Dieu, qu'on l'invoque à jamais!
Il nous donne ses lois, il se donne lui-même:
Pour tant de biens, il commande qu'on l'aime.
Miserere Domine!

Bow down thine ear, O Lord, hear me: for I am poor and needy. Preserve my soul: O thou my God, save thy servant that trusteth in thee. Be merciful unto me, O Lord: for I cry unto thee daily. Rejoice the soul of thy servant; for unto thee, O Lord, do I lift up my soul. For thou, Lord, art good, and ready to forgive; and plenteous in mercy unto all them that call upon thee. Give ear, O Lord, unto my prayer; and attend to the voice of my supplications.
Miserere Domine!

O Lord God of my salvation. I have cried day and night before thee: Let my prayer come before thee: incline thine ear unto my cry; for my soul is full of troubles; and my life draweth nigh unto the grave.
Miserere Domine!

Hear my prayer, O Lord, and let my cry come unto thee. Hide not thy face from me in the day when I am in trouble; incline thine ear unto me; in the day when I call answer me speedily. For my days are consumed like smoke, and my bones are burned as a hearth. My heart is smitten and withered like grass; I have eaten ashes like bread, and mingled my drink with weeping.

Miserere Domine!

Omnipotens sempiterne Deus, infirmitatem nostram propitius respice, atque ad protegendum nos dexteram tuæ majestatis extende.

Almighty, everlasting God, look with favor upon our weakness, and stretch forth the right hand of thy majesty to guard us.

Miserere Domine!

Præsta, quæsumus, omnipotens Deus, ut semper rationabilia meditantes, quæ tibi sunt placita et dictis exequamur et factis.

Grant, we beseech Thee, O Almighty God, that always thinking upon the things that are right, we may fulfil thy commandments both in word and deed.

Miserere Domine!

The Oratory

Benedicite omnia opera Domini Domino: laudate et superexaltate eum in sæcula.

O all ye Works of the Lord, bless ye the Lord; praise Him and magnify Him for ever!

Prayer does not stand high in the World's esteem. Pupils of science judge it a vain and foolish superstition. They may be quite right. But if there is no avail in prayer, neither is there in reason, in the cautious steps of the human intelligence from premises to conclusion; for denial of all value to prayer can only be on the assumption of determinism. If it merely rest on the denial of Deity, of a hearer, or of any power outside of man to alter the course of events, it is irrelevant; for a denial, to be of avail, must exclude the effect of prayer upon a man's self. To the seeker in his retreat, prayer is an exercise to strengthen the spirit, an unfolding of the soul's wings on a hoped-for flight, such as a skylark may take through cloud into sunshine beyond — a means of restoring equilibrium to the soul after tossing to and fro day by day in the rough crossings between sleep and sleep: the acquisition of indifferency to the pulls and tugs of appetite and pride, of impartiality between self and neighbor, of a balance that will weigh differences of

nationality, of class or creed; and an attainment
of the self-respect, the humility, of one who feels
that even he may serve the Lord, his God.

XIX
Spiritual Exercises

Plures reperiuntur contemplationem desiderare, sed quæ ad eam requiruntur, non student exercere.

Thomas à Kempis

IT is sometimes thought, by those who pay little heed to the matter, that the seeker after spiritual values leads an easy, effortless life, waiting for inspiration or a vision. On the contrary, in spiritual life as elsewhere, rewards are proportioned to labor, self-denial, and effort. It is not the idler, nor the self-indulgent man, that can withdraw his attention from the thousand glittering distractions which temptation spreads around, and fix his gaze steadfastly upward. The teachers of spiritual things, well knowing from their own experience the difficulties in the way, have drawn up a series of counsels to help the novice. Just as the student pursuing any discipline in a university, or an athlete bent upon becoming an oarsman or a football player, is directed and guided, so the student who wishes to learn what other men have believed to be spiritual knowledge, and to see what others have believed to be spiritual light, will follow the coun-

sels of the masters in his subject. No doubt there
are many roads, and each pilgrim must choose
his own according to his native bent and acquired
inclinations; but a retreat presents a definite philosophy of conduct, and for the solitary who is
honest in his search, the tabulated and codified
counsels of those that have attained should by no
means be neglected. According to the practice
of the main theological and ecclesiastical Christian tradition, these counsels lay down a plan of
spiritual exercises for daily use during the period
of the solitary's retreat or of his spiritual novitiate. These counsels are somewhat after this fashion. Let the novice banish all wandering fancies,
his mind following a certain train of thought,
very much as if he were attending service in a
metaphysical oratory within his own soul. There
is nothing out of the usual way in this: all religious sects and societies, whether for spiritual,
ethical, or mental health, have their liturgical
offices for prayer and meditation, in order to
stimulate and guide spiritual effort.

The novice begins by coming, as it were, to spiritual attention. *Adsum, Domine.* Then, his thoughts
collected, he utters some preparatory prayer:—

Help me, O Thou whom I blindly seek, to lay

aside whatever impulses and appetites of the World still cling to me: all envy of other men, all desire of Worldly success, all false doctrine of temporal good or of the World's satisfaction, all pride, all ill-will and self-deception, all hardness of heart, all vulgarity and self-love.

Next, preliminary to meditation, some phrase or ejaculation is to be taken from an approved poet or spiritual writer:—

Fili, Ego Dominus, confortans in die tribulationis; Venias ad me, cum tibi non fuerit bene.

My son, it is I, the Lord, ready to comfort in the day of tribulation; Come to me when thou art in trouble.

Subject of Meditation:

An episode taken from the life of Christ, or whomever the novice regards as the loftiest spiritual teacher:—

Jesus saith unto her, Mary. She turned herself and saith unto him, Rabboni; which is to say, Master. Jesus saith unto her, Touch me not; for I am not yet ascended to my Father: but go to my brethren, and say unto them, I ascend unto my Father, and your Father; and to my God and your God.

[133]

The novice is then directed to conjure up the scene before his mind's eye, as if he were recalling visual images that he had himself beheld.

The Episode, *according to the letter:*

Imagine yourself present. There before you kneels the woman worshiping and the Master stands denying. Imagine her woman's hands outstretched in supplication; imagine the Master's wounded feet that have trod the Syrian roads, the shores of Galilee, the regions round about Jerusalem, and at last the hard road up the hill of Golgotha. Imagine that you hear Mary's single word, and the Master's answering voice.

The Episode, *according to the Spirit:*

Human frailty kneels before the miraculous appearance of divine love. You are typified by Mary. Imagine yourself as filled with a passionate love of the Highest, and, in sudden forgetfulness of the truth that the Highest cannot be touched except after heroic self-mastery or self-abandonment, perhaps after suffering even unto death—you hope to attain to a knowledge and love of God by the mere outstretching of your hands. Holiness is out of a sinner's reach. You are permitted to behold the marks of the suf-

Spiritual Exercises

ferings that have enabled Holiness to realize itself, in order that you shall bear witness to your brethren that Holiness is of God, and that through holiness the human may hope at last to touch the Divine.

Meditation:

Life of my life, I shall ever try to keep my body pure, knowing that thy living touch is upon all my limbs.

I shall ever try to keep all untruths out from my thoughts, knowing that thou art that truth which has kindled the light of reason in my mind.

I shall ever try to drive all evils away from my heart and keep my love in flower, knowing that thou hast thy seat in the inmost shrine of my heart.

And it shall be my endeavor to reveal thee in my actions, knowing it is thy power gives me strength to act.

Prayer:

Grant me, O Thou whom I seek, the grace to know what men can know of thy truth, and the will to seek after thy Holy Spirit.

Meditative sequences:

taken from the Bible, Thomas à Kempis, or any sacred poet or writer in some way connected with

[135]

the main subject of meditation. For instance, the cross as symbol of purification through suffering:—

He that taketh not his cross, and followeth after me, is not worthy of me.

If thou bearest the cross willingly, it will bear thee and bring thee to thy wished-for end.

If thou bearest it unwillingly, thou makest it a burden, and still thou must bear it.

Dost thou think thou canst escape that which no mortal could ever avoid? What saint was ever in the world that did not bear his cross and tribulation?

Needs must that Christ suffered; and how is it that thou wilt seek a way other than this royal road, which is the way of the holy cross?

The life of Christ was a cross and a martyrdom; and dost thou seek for thyself rest and joy?

Erras, Erras, si aliud quæris, quam pati tribulationes: quia tota ista vita mortalis, plena est miseriis, et circumsignata crucibus.

You go astray, astray, if you seek for aught else than to suffer tribulation: for all this mortal life is full of sorrows, and crosses fence it round about.

And the higher thou shalt attain in spirit, so

much the heavier shalt thou find thy cross; the
pain of exile shall grow greater with thy greater
love.

And yet though thou art afflicted in manifold
ways, thou shalt not lack some intermixture of
consolation; for thou shalt become aware of the
rich harvest sprouting within thee that grows
from the suffering of the cross.

For if thou shalt willingly bend beneath it, all
the heaviness of tribulation will turn into trust in
the divine compassion.

Resolution:

This day, and to-morrow and to-morrow, I will
construct before my inward eye, my inward ear,
my inward folded hands, an image of holiness.
Toward this I will aspire.

Beati mundo corde.

Amen.

XX

𝕮𝖍𝖊 𝖀𝖘𝖚𝖆𝖑 𝕽𝖊𝖕𝖗𝖔𝖆𝖈𝖍

"Lo sol sen va," soggiunse, "e vien la sera:
non v'arrestate, ma studiate il passo,
mentre che l'occidente non s'annera."
Purgatorio, xxvii, 61//3

THE other regulations for other hours of the day I may pass over lightly. If our Solitary lives in a monastery, he will, at meals, listen to what lections the prior may deem fit; but if he live in a hermitage, or have a table to himself, it is well for him to have some book quite different from the solemn books of his severer studies. He will do well to read comedy. If there be a God, He is God of laughter as well as of tears; Christianity has gone astray in worshiping its God solely as a Man of Sorrows. A universal God must enter at the door of grief, but he must also enter by the door of heart-easing mirth. On the book-rest upon his table, just to the left of his plate, let the recluse put a volume of Molière, Cowper's Letters, Goldoni, Henri Meilhac, or such a delightful little play as *Lo es posible*, or the *Vicar of Wakefield*, *Poil de Carotte*, *Il Piccolo Mondo Antico*, *Le Journal de Madame de La Tour du Pin*, or *Tartarin de*

[138]

Tarascon. Of such books *Don Quixote* is the non-pareil. But the recluse must consult his taste, and if he finds in light comedy or farce too tart a contrast with his habitual thoughts, let him read Izaak Walton's *Lives*, *Port Royal*, *The Journal* of John Woolman, or Tolstoi's *Confessions*, or any such.

And in the evening, seated in his room, gazing at the patch of sky bounded by his window-frame, or pacing the silent garden path, he must, under the rules, give himself over to contemplation for the period of half an hour. Let him abstract himself from things of sense, push fancies and memories aside, narrow more and more his field of consciousness, and finally draw his attention in toward the centre, until he fix it as best he may upon some single point at the very heart of his deepest desire; let him lose self, if not in ecstasy like some Christian mystics, at least on the ethereal summits of untroubled serenity. Surely the Buddha Gautama helped his fellows to deliverance from woe, from vulgarity, from the illusions of the World's teachings.

Such then, in brief, are the ways of life in a retreat to-day, for the penitent who desires to profit by the methods of Christian tradition and to spare

himself the labyrinthine difficulties of finding
the right road by himself.

Not everybody can profit by a retreat, not
everybody wishes to; and yet the very unwillingness of children of the World to reconsider
the values that the World teaches them is a reason for such reconsideration; just as it is good
for young men born and bred in one country
to travel and acquaint themselves with the ways
and thoughts of other nations, since they may
learn that ideas and beliefs which they had been
taught at home to accept as standards for all humanity, need to be, in the interests of humanity and of themselves, reëxamined and rejudged.
The pursuit of inward peace, the conquest of the
bodily appetites, the cultivation of self-renuncia-
tion, reverence, aspiration, and whatever fruits
of the spirit may be gathered from the tree of
self-consecration — these are desirable, and they
should be sought systematically. For the purpose of such systematic teaching, retreats have
been established; they are spiritual schools, and
of many kinds. In some, pupils teach themselves; in others, they are directed. When St.
Catherine of Siena was forbidden by her parents
to retire to her bedchamber to worship, she made
a cell within her soul to which she withdrew for

prayers and sacred thoughts. St. François de
Sales says, that as birds fly to their nests, and
deer seek the shady recesses of the forest, so human beings in the very thick of worldly affairs
or social frivolity should withdraw for however
short a time into the privacy of their own souls.
St. Catherine and those penitents whom St. François de Sales advised were not free to forsake the
world; but for such as were, ancient tradition, ac-
cepting the example of Christ and the Hebrew
prophets, counseled a retreat of forty days in the
desert. St. Ignatius Loyola prescribed thirty for
the practice of his spiritual exercises. Modern
spiritual directors consult the circumstances of
their penitents. But in the matter of retreats, as in
other human affairs, it is always easier to do what
others have done than to make a way for oneself,
and a man seesawing between yes and no will
often follow another's example; such hesitants
need the countenance and encouragement that
radiate from men who devote their whole lives
to the contemplative virtues. Life-long recluses,
in the nature of things, can never number more
than a handful, even of such as are discontent
with the aims and interests of the World. But the
footprints of a single man may point the path to a
multitude that have lost their way; and it might

well be that the bare vision of a recluse living
in some sequestered spot, frugal, self-denying,
practising the contemplative virtues, indifferent
to material welfare and social consideration, and
radiantly serene, would persuade two or three,
or five or ten, to practise a retreat for a time. For
the sake of such persuasion it might be worth
while for men weary of the World, or born without a taste for it, to become in some modern
fashion out-and-out monks or hermits. What if
their doing so should be foolishness in the eyes
of the World, and a stumbling-block to many
who are trying in their own way to reform the
World from within? Is it not worth while for
men of ascetic beliefs to run risks, or even to
sacrifice themselves, for a high hope? Men are
sacrificed in the World every day for causes far
less meritorious. What if the reformers within
the World protest, as reformers will, against
reforms that do not wear their brand? The needs
of humanity justify any honest experiment. Let
us look about us: at the wars between nations,
the struggle between classes, the selfishness of
the rich, the intemperance of the poor, the want,
sickness, sin, that abound, the vice that pollutes
city, village, and, it is said, remote farmhouses,—
to such a degree that were the comfortably off by

some evil fate thin-skinned they could not endure it,—the bickering between Christian sects
and all the ills that come because we do not follow the teachings of Jesus of Nazareth. Does not
this spectacle justify any experiment, even the
revival of mediæval methods, in the hope to
persuade men to do what Jesus bade? And the
principles of the retreat are not without creden-
tials; they are warranted by the self-denial, the
self-effacement, the self-consecration of the recluse and the solitary.

Here let me say a word as to the usual reproach addressed to solitaries. The World charges
them with selfishness. I raise no question as to
whether the World might better confine this criticism to its own members; I only ask, in what
respect recluses or hermits are more selfish in
their attitude toward the World than the World
in its attitude toward them? The World wishes
the recluse to renounce his creed, to come back,
take his place in the turmoil of business and
pleasure, do as the World does, help pile the
bricks and lay the girders of its Tower of Babel.
Is this unselfishness on its part? The World
reiterates that the recluse belongs to the same
species as itself, to the same race, nation, clan,
and as such has social duties; but because the

World is gregarious and follows the ethics of
the herd, must solitaries fall in line, like sheep,
and do as others do? Beyond question this gregarious morality has been of marked service in the
long interracial struggle for physical existence,
by holding together the members of the group,
for defence or attack, and in economic matters,
though at an immense cost of individual self-
sacrifice. But the goal of this system is the triumph of species, race, or nation; and the brightest
prospect of the achievement of such triumph
leaves the recluse cold and indifferent. For him,
the system is a mere social policy, wise for the
mass of men, but not of universal obligation.
Why, then, should he accept the World's ethics?
The World is no more within its rights when it
bids the recluse wear its livery than the recluse
would be within his were he to ask the World to
follow Schopenhauer and reject the will-to-live.

For the recluse each man lies under a personal
responsibility for what, in the old phrase, he calls
the salvation of his soul; and though it is his
duty to consult as wide an experience as he can
before he constructs his theory of salvation, he
must nevertheless construct that theory for himself. If it be thrown up against him that in re-
jecting gregarious morality he is advocating sel-

fishness as against altruism, I can only say that
in all the monks or hermits of whom I have
read—I speak of such as have become monks or
hermits from inner conviction and not in obedience to custom, or love of ease, or any species
of shirking—I have found a degree of unselfishness rarely to be matched among secular persons.
The recluse believes in unselfishness, but he finds
the sanction elsewhere than in ancestral habits; he
hopes, however frail that hope, however wrapped
about by darkness, that unselfishness receives
the sanction of the good pleasure of God. He is
vague, of course, mystical, irrational, in his speculation. He believes—if fantastic, iridescent,
ever shifting, vaporous images of beauty may be
called belief—in the spiritual, by which he means
the true interests of the soul: everlasting if the
soul is everlasting, temporary if the soul is limited in time. And his awkward attempt to dis-
tinguish the spiritual from the ethical, as ethics
are usually accepted, lies in this, that ethics seem
to find their sanction in the welfare, or reputed
welfare, of the tribe, or at amplest, of the human
race; whereas the spiritual, as he dares to hope,
depends for its sanction on a love and knowledge of a divine will. And his answer to the
perpetual reiterations of the World that his very

hopes, thoughts, yearnings, consciousness, are social products, like his food, is that he recks not who grew the grain, or ground the corn, or baked the bread, but merely whether it will satisfy his hunger. He will not believe that his deepest affections are merely animal instincts, whatever their origin, nor that his yearning for God is merely an imperfect organization in the cells and fibres of his brain.

These suggestions are but frontier defences; the citadel of his position is this: that humanity is the larger circle that embraces both the recluse and the World. Let the monks build their monasteries in the Alps, the Apennines, the Andes, or the Himalayas, or the hermit find his cave or pitch his tent where he will, neither they nor he are without influence upon the World, or unrelated to its inhabitants. The archetypes, St. Anthony and St. Benedict, are evidence enough. There is not a hermit but of him some one may say,

> Oft have we seen him at the peep of dawn
> Brushing with hasty steps the dews away,

and they that see him go their ways with some new reflections concerning life, some fresh examination of the things they live by. When they

pass a house of retreat perhaps they perceive a
quietness that they do not find at home, perhaps
they scent the fragrance of the garden, perhaps
they hear the note of an organ or the words of
a psalm, perhaps they find those within, though
with none of the possessions that they call good,
serene and calm. Honest seekers of spiritual peace
are justified by their works. No man can save his
own soul without necessarily helping his brother
save his soul likewise.

XXI
The Great Human Need

An highway shall be there . . . and
it shall be called the way of holiness.
Isaiah, xxxv: 8

NE more word. If it is sure and indubitable that there is a God, then it is sure and indubitable that some body of men should set themselves apart, whether for life or for a season, to seek a knowledge of Him and of his will, in ways quite different from those in which dwellers in the World seek Him, supposing that some dwellers in the World do really seek Him. For even if this segregated body makes no discovery, reaches no port, and seems to sail over the high seas of thought and hope in vain, nevertheless no voyage of discovery is wholly fruitless, for like other seekers after knowledge these adventurers render a general service by the elimination of wrong courses and erroneous hypotheses. They bestow upon men the hope that the routes of error are being crossed off the old charts of life and that the chances of attainment grow brighter and brighter.

If it is doubtful whether there be a God or

no, it is still of equal importance that a search be made, that seekers scatter abroad and look in all directions, study their own hearts, examine things metaphysical, ponder upon ecstasy and rapture and the passionate love of the infinite that possesses the souls of men now and again. There are enough students, philosophers, savants in the World to investigate the laws of matter, the ways of organic life, and track the flying footprints of Nature into her deepest recesses.

But let us suppose that it is sure and indubitable that there is no God, that the World is right, that motion in space is the ultimate truth, and that in the search of truth the methods of science are the only methods: that what science busies itself with is the only thing to busy oneself with. Nevertheless, as I think, the need of the contemplative and the solitary will become all the greater. If the formation of crystals, the habits of bees, the usages, affections, and thoughts of men, are all on one level of significance, all mere varying records of chance throbbings of some irrational, unintelligent power, if there is no further truth beyond some possible door, then men must take account of this situation, and do what little may be in their power to improve it. The hypothesis assumes that truth has no claim

[149]

to any of the solemnity, the devout service, the reverence that the religious attitude of mind has invested it with; the inmost shrine of truth, to borrow an ancient phrase, has no more title to respect than the smoking-room of a Pullman car; beauty deserves no worship; the sacred, the sublime, are mere antiquated names to conceal ignorance, to designate that which shall one day, when knowledge progresses still further, become common, commonplace, vulgar. Love, at its height, is no more than the exuberant and excessive development of the primary instincts. Such is the situation which, under the hypothesis, we confront.

The element in the situation that in especial concerns the subject of this brief is that, explain it as we may, — for the explanation, whatever it should be, is immaterial, — man has a need of something holy. He has become accustomed to a theory that there is some supreme goal toward which he should set his face; that the love of the mother for her son, of David for Absalom, of Dante for Beatrice, of St. Augustine for his God, are somehow rays that shine from out the clouds which veil the goal; and that truth and beauty likewise are beams. To find some makeshift is now his task. Holiness has become a need, his deepest most abiding need, and he cannot ignore

it. Without the possibility of a God, our backs
are to the wall, and we must make an heroic effort
to confront reality.

The need of holiness, perhaps, will not be
granted. But I shall assume it. And, as there is
nothing known to us in the universe higher than
man, I assume that holiness must be created out
of the ideas and out of the lives of men. I assume
that the type of man called holy is needful to
men, that his holiness is of a value to be set beside
the capacity of the master of a great industry,
the ingenuity of a man of science, the creative-
ness of an artist. Such a type, without belief in
a God, will be difficult; but this is a difficulty to
which men must address themselves. If I may
compare that which we are accustomed to call the
spiritual with an idea evolved in the most worldly
class in society, the idea of holiness is not without similarity to the idea of honor. The similarity lies in this: Honor, in the antiquated significance of the word, is a fantastic, irrational
idea, which was, if not created, at least cultivated
by men of a certain special education, men in-
stilled in early youth with certain definite dogmas, trained to accept certain values, disciplined
to act with unquestioning obedience to their
creed. This creed constrained them to perform

actions which lie beyond the range of self-interest—as self-interest is interpreted in the theories which cluster around the hypothesis that life
is a battle for the preservation of self—and to
conduct themselves in a manner that does not fit
into the usual interpretation of the good of the
race. The men who accepted this creed and acted
upon it were called gentlemen. It is quite apart
from the parallel suggested, that the limitations,
the essential wrongness, of the creed, be granted
or disputed. The creed has exerted a very marked
influence, and even now, perhaps, a man would
regard as the strongest possible mode of affirmation the statement made upon his honor.

As with the idea of honor, so it is with the
idea of holiness; a special class, a special training, a special obedience, are necessary to produce
and maintain this sentiment. In order to supply the spiritual needs of men,— I am speaking
under the hypothesis that there is no God, no life
hereafter, no soul apart from the nervous system,—a definite, unquestioned, imperious dogma
that holiness is a sort of spiritual honor must be
created. It must be fashioned out of a material,
matched with which the tertiary rocks of the
Laurentian Mountains are easily shaped to the
craftsman's will; it must be wrought out of ideas

that exclude the divine, and out of a godless life. The requisite art to deal with such material demands a sort of spiritual workshop or studio, in which the craftsmen shall go to school. And how can this be done in the World, where men are struggling for money and prodigal in spending it, where there is making love and marrying, the pursuit of notoriety, office, fame, or whatever else ambition may desire? How in such a hubbub can poor human nature hold itself free from discontent, envy, vexation, disappointment, covetousness, lust, greed, malice, and all the contaminations that mar and stain the innocence of holiness? How in such confusion is it possible to secure renunciation, serenity, selflessness, indifference to outward things, or, most of all, concentration upon one single end? This is not, of course, to deny that many virtues are wrought in the World — energy, courage, love of justice and mercy, and the great human affections — and best wrought in the World. And yet how seldom, how very seldom, have any of these virtues appeared in secular life unspotted by injustice, by prejudice, by intemperance of thought, of speech and act, by desire for praise, by the self-love inseparable from the pursuit of any worldly end! As the far-seeing poet says, "Es bildet ein Talent sich in der Stille," and holiness demands a talent, many talents, of a special sort, and these can be developed only in solitude.

No doubt there is, if one wishes to put it in this way, a taste for holiness just as there is a taste for refinement, whether in art, in literature, or in conduct; and just as parents and school-masters endeavor to implant in the young a taste for virtue, so it should be possible to implant in some among them a taste for holiness. Such a taste would never be universal, it would not be popular; but love of refinement is not universal, not even popular, and the same holds good concerning beauty. If one will but reflect how great a part authority plays in our education, our customs, our religion, one need not be incredulous as to the possibility of establishing a taste for holiness, of calling out talents to develop that taste, and also of securing means to cultivate such talents.

Because monks in their seclusion and hermits in their solitude tried of old to achieve holiness and failed—if indeed they failed—is of no great weight as an argument that men should not try seclusion and solitude again. In the times when men believed in a God, it was possible to contend that God might be in every place, as well

[154]

in the World as out of it; but now, under the hypothesis, we recognize that holiness is a sentiment, a taste, a work of art, and therefore it plainly requires a great effort of social and individual volition. Let men strive for it in the World if they can be persuaded thereto; but let other ways be tried as well. Let lonely souls go off by themselves, and let the World feel that out of solitude may come a light that shall help many along their way.

The sun is set, the moon no longer shines, no stars twinkle in the sky; we must light our candles, or we shall be in utter darkness.

The End

Appendix

Appendix

OPENING

> Thou that see'st my evil ways, worthless, undutiful,
>   Lord of the heavens, unseen, immortal,
>   Succour my frail and erring soul,
>   And with thy grace fill up its emptiness:
> So, though I've lived in warfare and in storm,
>   That I may die in peace and port; and though my life
>   Was vain, at least be my parting good.
> For the short time of stay that still remains,
>   And at my death, grant that thy hand be nigh,
>   Thou knowest well I have no hope elsewhere.
>
> *Petrarch*

I will speak to the Lord, although I am dust and ashes.
Thomas à Kempis

My Son, thou canst not attain perfect freedom unless thou
wholly deny thyself. *Thomas à Kempis*

CHAPTER I

HEADING: *It is not given to all men to forsake all things, renounce the
World, and adopt a monastic life.*

Of the World, St. François de Sales says : Qu'est-ce que le
monde ? Le monde se doit entendre de ceux qui ont une affection déréglée aux biens, à la vie, aux honneurs, dignités, préémi-
nences, propre estime, et semblables bagatelles après lesquelles
tout les mondains courent et s'en rendent idolâtres.
Sermon pour la Nativité de Notre Dame

And Pascal : L'homme est visiblement fait pour penser ; c'est
toute sa dignité et tout son mérite, et tout son devoir est de
penser comme il faut : or l'ordre de la pensée est de commencer
par soi, et par son auteur et sa fin.

Or, à quoi pense le monde ? Jamais à cela; mais à danser, à jouer du luth, à chanter, à faire des vers, à courir la bague, *etc.*

Pensées, Art. xviii, 12

CHAPTER II

Heading: *And I saw this world in such guise that I smiled at its cheap appearance.*

Pascal says : En voyant l'aveuglement et la misère de l'homme (et ces contrariétés étonnantes qui se découvrent dans sa nature), en regardant tout l'univers muet, et l'homme sans lumière, abandonné à lui-même, et comme égaré dans ce recoin de l'univers, sans savoir qui l'y a mis, ce qu'il y est venu faire, ce qu'il deviendra en mourant, incapable de toute connaissance, j'entre en effroi comme un homme qu'on aurait porté endormi dans une île déserte et effroyable, et qui s'éveilleroit sans connaître où il est, et sans moyen d'en sortir. *Pensées,* Art. vi, 1

CHAPTER III

Heading: *Little children, keep yourselves from idols.*

The quotation concerning Socrates is from the *Phædo* 79.

Lord Bacon says : A recluse leaves the world out of a love and desire to sequester a man's self for a higher conversation.

Essays

Fénelon: Si vous voulez aimer Dieu, pourquoi voulez-vous passer votre vie dans l'amitié de ceux qui ne l'aiment pas et qui se moquent de son amour ? *Lettres Spirituelles, No.* 1

CHAPTER IV

Heading: *They were strangers to the World, but very close familiar friends to God. — Thomas à Kempis*

Eugénie de Guérin was born in 1805 and died in 1848. She lived in Cayla, a little place in southern France. Her *Journal* was published in 1862, her *Lettres* in 1864; Sainte-Beuve and Matthew Arnold made her known to the public.

Appendix

CHAPTER V

St. Anthony was an Egyptian Saint, who died at a great age about 356 A.D.

CHAPTER VI

HEADING: *O Lord, grant them eternal rest, and let light everlasting shine upon them.* (*Benedictine motto*)

St. Benedict, 480–543 A.D., born in Nursia, Umbria. He founded the monastic system of western Europe. St. Gregory the Great wrote his life. See, Cuthbert Butler, *Benedictine Monachism* and *Benedicti Regula*, and Dom Germain Morin, *L'Idéal Monastique et la Vie Chrétienne des premiers jours.*

CHAPTER VII

HEADING: *O whosoever had a spark of true love would perceive at once that all worldly things are full of vanity.*—*Thomas à Kempis*

Thomas à Kempis, 1380–1471, was a German monk who spent most of his life in the monastery of St. Agnes, near the town of Zwolle in the Netherlands.

CHAPTER VIII

HEADING: *My Son, what is this thing or that to thee? Follow thou Me.*—*Thomas à Kempis.*

Senancour, 1770–1846. Author of *Libres méditations d'un solitaire inconnu, Obermann*, etc. He became known to English readers by Matthew Arnold's poem, *Obermann*.

Amiel, 1821–1881, A Swiss scholar. His *Journal* was published after his death; his poems, which are less well known, were published in his lifetime.

Appendix

CHAPTER IX

HEADING: *But they that follow Thee from contempt of worldly things and in mortification of the flesh, show themselves to be truly wise; for they have passed from vanity to truth, from flesh to the spirit*

Thomas à Kempis

CHAPTER X

See, *e.g.*, A. J. Balfour's *Humanism and Theism.*

CHAPTER XI

The quotations from Thoreau are taken from his *Journal.*

CHAPTER XIII

> O Virgin, if ever tenderest pity
> For mortal things moved thee to mercy,
> Incline unto my prayer;
> Save me in this deadly strife,
> Though I am clay, and thou
> Of Heaven the Queen.
>
> *Petrarch*

CHAPTER XIV

HEADING: *Passing on into the state and freedom of the children of God, who stand above the present and fix their eyes upon eternal things.* — *Thomas à Kempis*

Iliad, Book XVI.

Plato, *The Apology.*

CHAPTER XV

HEADING: *There is a gentle lady in heaven.* — *Inferno, ii,* 94

> The mother dolorous was standing
> Next the cross a-weeping
> While her son hung there;

[162]

Appendix

Her groaning heart,
In suffering and agony,
The sword had pierced.

Sir Oliver Lodge, whose reputation as a man of science has procured him a hearing for many strange theories, says: The idea of *Angels* is usually treated as fanciful. Imaginative it is, but not altogether fanciful; and though the physical appearance and attributes of such imaginary beings may have been overemphasized or misconceived, yet facts known to me indicate that we are not really lonely in our struggle, that our destiny is not left to haphazard, that there is no such thing as *laissez-faire* in a highly organized universe. Help may be rejected, but help is available; a ministry of benevolence surrounds us—a cloud of witnesses—not witnesses only but helpers, agents like ourselves of the immanent God.

Reason and Belief

CHAPTER XVII

HEADING: *I am the light of the world: he that followeth me shall not walk in darkness, but shall have the light of life.*

Philosophy directs us to that spiritual reality which is the only reality; and from this point of view philosophy and religion are one.   *J. S. Haldane, Mechanism, Life and Personality*

CHAPTER XVIII

These prayers are taken from St. Augustine, Jeremy Taylor, Christina Rossetti, Dante, Racine, the Psalms, the *Breviarium Romanum*, the *Benedicite*, etc.

CHAPTER XIX

HEADING: *There are many to be found that wish to be able to contemplate, but they heed not to practise that which is necessary for contemplation.*—*Thomas à Kempis*

These spiritual exercises are based on those of St. Ignatius Loyola.

[163]

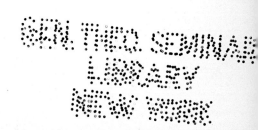

Appendix

The meditation is from Tagore's *Gitanali.*

The meditative sequences are from *The Imitation of Christ.*

CHAPTER XX

HEADING:

"*The sun is setting and the evening comes,*"
He said, "*Tarry not, but hasten on,*
While the west is not yet dark."

CHAPTER XXI

Goethe: Talent is fashioned in retirement.   *Torquato Tasso*

Nietszche says: I have gradually come to see daylight in regard to the most general defect in our methods of education and training: nobody learns, nobody teaches, nobody wishes to endure solitude. (Niemand lernt, Niemand strebt darnach, Niemand lehrt die Einsamkeit ertragen.)   *The Dawn of Day*

We retire into seclusion . . . so that by retirement we may collect and save forces which will some day be urgently needed by civilization. . . . We make capital and try to safeguard it.

Human, All Too Human

The number of petty vengeful people, and, even more, the number of their petty acts of revenge, is incalculable. The air around us is continually whizzing with arrows discharged by their malignity, so that the sun and sky of their lives are darkened by them — and, alas! not only theirs, but more often ours . . . and this is worse than the frequent wounds they inflict upon our skins and hearts. . . . Well then, Solitude: because of this, Solitude!   *The Dawn of Day*

Le malheur des hommes vient d'une seule chose qui est de ne savoir pas demeurer en repos dans une chambre.
Pascal, *Pensées,* Art. XXI, I

[164]

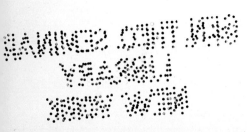